THE MISSING LINKS

America's Greatest Lost Golf Courses & Holes

DANIEL WEXLER

Sleeping Bear Press

PUBLISHER

Sleeping Bear Press
310 North Main
P.O. Box 20
Chelsea, Michigan 48118
www.sleepingbearpress.com

Printed and bound in Canada.
10 9 8 7 6 5 4 3 2 1

Library of Congress Cataloging-in-Publication Data

Wexler, Daniel.
The missing links : lost golf courses and holes / by Daniel Wexler.
p. cm.
ISBN 1-886947-60-0
1. Golf courses-United States-Design and construction-History. 2. Golf course architects-United States-History. I . Title.

GV981 .W48 2000
796.352'06'873-dc21
99-087515

For those with the courage to defend this great game
against the scourge of profit-motivated technology, and
for David Marr, one of golf's truly fine gentlemen.

TABLE OF CONTENTS

INTRODUCTION

Why a book on golf courses that no longer exist?

The answer began to take shape several years ago while I was researching a project on the evolution of America's classic courses and, novelty potential in mind, considered including Charles Blair Macdonald's long-lost Lido Golf Club in Lido Beach, New York. Several months later, when the late David Marr was kind enough to review a list of my prospective courses, the excitement was palpable in his voice when he came to The Lido. "Claude Harmon once told me," he gushed in his wonderful Texas drawl, "that The Lido was the greatest golf course ever."

Hmm...

Looking back, it took longer than it probably should have to convert that book idea into this one. Sure, I thought, The Lido may have been great but, in general, if a course was any good wouldn't it still be with us?

Enter Geoffrey Cornish and Ron Whitten's seminal volume *The Architects Of Golf*. For here was a book which endeavored to catalogue all that has been done in course design, an improbably large task. My curiosity aroused, I sat down and drew up a list of all the defunct facilities credited to perhaps a dozen of golf's classic architects, those practicing during the field's pre-World War II Golden Age. To my astonishment, that list came to over 100, and suddenly the game was on.

In the course of researching this volume I have discovered several fascinating things about lost courses. First, with the popularity of Golden Age designs ever growing, it has been exciting to uncover—in some cases to be the first set of eyes in decades to see—the forgotten works of the great masters. Sort of like rediscovering a lost Rembrandt I suppose, only in this case I got to rediscover dozens.

Second, I am reminded of Ben Crenshaw's foreword to my friend Geoff Shackelford's wonderful biography of legendary architect George Thomas, *The Captain*. Speaking of golf design, Crenshaw writes:

"Consider the scale of its very proportions, its lasting contributions on such vast canvasses."

And indeed one realizes that a golf course is not a framed painting hung upon some wall but a living, breathing, 150-acre entity; an undertaking of enormous size; a sculpture of massive, community-altering proportion. When a golf course vanishes (generally to be subdivided into hundreds of residential dwellings) an entire area changes—and not just ecologically.

Of course, it is precisely the need for such change that did so many of these fine courses in. I, like many of you I'll bet, originally assumed that it was economic hardship brought on by the Depression or the second World War that killed these clubs, but just as frequently it was America's massive postwar suburban expansion. Courses originally laid out on the outskirts of town suddenly found themselves engulfed by the inexorable sprawl of "progress," driving their property taxes up, making the lucrative offers of hungry developers seem all the more enticing.

Sell your in-town land at a profit, purchase a new tract farther out, build yourself a modern, "state-of-the-art" facility, then kick back and enjoy it for however many years you may have before constant population growth mandates a repetition of the entire cycle. Realistic, profitable, perhaps even necessary, but from a golfing point of view ravaged by one fatal flaw: postwar America was, in golf architecture terms, a relative wasteland, resulting in oh so many suburban clubs which were, like 1970s and '80s baseball stadiums, completely interchangeable from cookie cutters.

Just plain dull.

So how good were these lost originals? Read this book and you can decide for yourself. But I will offer this opinion: judged objectively, at least six or seven would comfortably crack today's "Top 100," with such gems as The Lido and Timber Point pushing high up toward the top of the list. Factor in the ever-growing favor that so many Golden Age classics are finding among ratings panelists, and the overall Top 100 number might well rise as high as a dozen.

With this in mind, I have chosen to feature 27 of the finest lost facilities, providing for each a complete map and scorecard, extensive description, and some sense of how the layout might measure up in the length-and toughness-oriented golf world of today. Additionally, for the premier architects I have included sidebars discussing most of their other lost works, offering as many maps, pictures, and descriptions as space will allow.

Finally, I offer several important notes.

First, at the risk of stating the obvious, it is important to remember that the vast majority of these prewar designs played quite a bit shorter than most modern courses, but in direct proportion to the equipment of the era. Their Golden Age brethren which have survived were little different. They have simply grown steadily throughout the intervening years.

Second, while the maps appearing in this volume have been prepared as accurately as possible, the vagaries of dated material and the tendency of early architects to vary their plans significantly in the field have occasionally made an exact presentation difficult. Similarly, such traditional sources as aerial photos or course drawings seldom offer any sense of green contouring, a vital aspect of any golf course's playability and design. The reader may rest assured, however, that each drawing has been verified against all available sources with yardages taken, wherever possible, from actual club scorecards.

Finally, one mild disclaimer. It has been my hope throughout the research process to clean up completely whatever erroneous information has previously appeared regarding the lost designs of the great architects. To that end I have contacted a myriad of local, regional, and national sources from coast to coast, and while I do not suggest that my results are 100% perfect, I am confident that they are the most dependable yet assembled. Still, it is my sincere hope that information possessed by readers that either refutes or builds upon this material might be brought to my attention, both for a matter of record and for the correctness of future works.

I give you then *America's Missing Links*, a group profoundly worthy of our study and emulation, and to whose glory, I trust, this volume will prove a fair and admiring toast.

Daniel Wexler
Los Angeles, CA

CHARLES BANKS

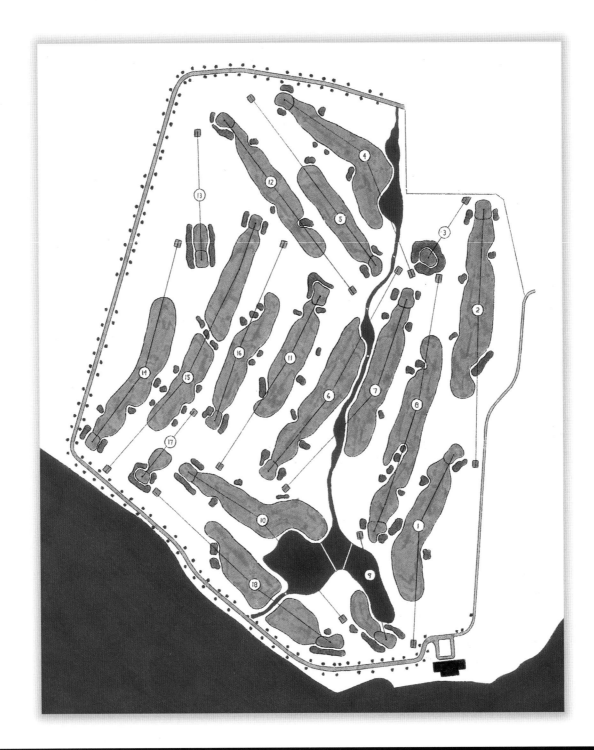

WESTHAMPTON (Oneck)																				
380	450	150	400	380	420	420	470	190	3260	420	360	390	220	400	550	350	160	430	3280	6540
4	4	3	4	4	4	4	5	3	35	4	4	4	3	4	5	4	3	4	35	70

WESTHAMPTON COUNTRY CLUB

WESTHAMPTON, NY

Oneck Course, 1929 / 6,540 yards Par-70

Throughout history there have been countless examples of young, talented people furthering their careers by studying at the hand of a master. On rare occasions, such up-and-comers have even experienced the good fortune of working with a genuine pioneer, enjoying a uniquely direct lineage to the very roots of their chosen endeavor. One such example: the Hall-of-Fame basketball coach Dean Smith who was coached at the University of Kansas by Phog Allen, who in turn had been coached by Dr. James Naismith, the very inventor of the sport.

If a similar scenario ever played itself out in the field of golf course architecture, it would surely have been in the person of Mr. Charles Banks, teacher, headmaster, and final heir to the design dynasty begun by the discipline's American mentor, Mr. Charles Blair Macdonald. For Banks, the connection to Macdonald ran through Seth Raynor, C.B.'s longstanding right-hand and himself a designer of rare talent. The time of their meeting was 1920, the place, the Hotchkiss School in Lakeville, Connecticut, where Banks was Headmaster and Raynor was building the school's new golf course. The two men became friends, Banks became involved in the layout's construction, and soon thereafter renounced his career in academia to pursue golf architecture full-time.

By working closely with Raynor and Macdonald, Banks inherited not just their contacts but also their distinctive style of design, a technique involving the frequent replication of great holes from the British Isles. Like most successful disciples, however, he succeeded in placing his own stamp of individuality upon it, earning the nickname "Steamshovel" for the degree to which he built up his green complexes and excavated bunkers of sometimes staggering depth.

Unlike many designers of the Golden Age, Banks was fortunate in that nearly all of his significant designs have survived into the modern era, the notable exception being the Oneck Course of the Westhampton Country Club.

It can be argued that given the history of golf in the area, Banks was the only reasonable choice for the Oneck commission. Macdonald, after all, had defined the future of golf design with his landmark National Golf Links of America in nearby Southampton in 1911. Later, both he and Raynor did extensive additional local work, including Raynor's solo effort on the Westhampton club's first layout in 1915. By the time the club was ready to expand in 1929, however, Raynor was deceased and Macdonald retired, leaving Banks (whose ads of the period frequently read "SPECIALIZING IN THE RAYNOR TYPE OF COURSE") as the obvious remaining option.

Banks himself cited the quality of the Oneck Point property in a 1930 *The American Golfer* piece, noting its "over one thousand and seven hundred feet of shore frontage, a factor which makes the course attractive and cool, and which makes the property valuable." The same article also pointed out that over 500,000 cubic yards of sand were carted in to convert a great deal of marshland into usable golfing terrain. Though environmentally unfeasible today, such carte blanche in shaping the land was obviously appealing, allowing the architect the relative freedom to create whatever features he desired.

Facing the clearly-defined task of building "one of the finest courses on Long Island," Banks responded with a beauty: a 6,540-yard test which, playing to a wind-rattled par of 70, was enough to challenge even the elite players of the day.

The layout began with a fairly basic 380-yard opener, followed by a long 450-yard par-4 generally aided substantially by the prevailing breeze.

The third hole, measuring only 150 yards, was likely a replica of Macdonald's original Short hole at The National, and it is here that Banks' professional lineage becomes relevant. For as we shall see later on, it was the habit of Macdonald and Raynor to slip some variety into their replicas, making changes suitable to a given landscape while retaining the fundamental challenge and aesthetics central to each hole's architectural greatness. In the case of the Short, those challenges included a green surrounded by sand and a horseshoe-shaped contour built within the putting surface. This contour was generally quite pronounced, channeling well-struck shots toward the hole while repelling mediocre efforts to the outer reaches of the putting surface.

The fourth was a strong 400-yarder, made interesting by one's first encounter with a meandering water hazard (actually connected to Moriches Bay) that would work its way prominently into play on five more occasions. Here it angled up the right side, menacing the weak slice but generally not affecting the better player.

Following the straightaway fifth came a pair of long and particularly challenging par-4s, their back-and-forth configuration allowing the brook to closely guard the left side of each.

1938 aerial survey of the Oneck course, five years after its closing. Road and
Redan greens, and most Banks' bunkering still visible. (National Archives)

At 470 yards, the eighth was Westhampton's first par-5, and its relative shortness should not be deceiving. Routed directly into the wind, it was menaced by four diagonal bunkers in the landing area of the second shot, and a green complex flashing touches of a favored Raynor/Banks look, the squarish putting surface.

The outward half closed with a Banks rendition of the most copied hole in golf, the Redan. Based on the 193-yard 15th at North Berwick in Scotland, the Redan's challenge is created primarily by a green which falls away prominently back-left, a side of the putting surface always fronted by a deep, intimidating bunker. For the smart player the obvious shot is toward the right-center, allowing the green's substantial contour to release the ball naturally toward the hole. For the less-cerebral, a ball aimed back-left will generally skip long or worse, find the ever-dangerous Redan bunker. This 190-yard Banks version added a slight flourish: 165-yard carry over water first.

The Oneck Course's back nine began with one of its finest two-shotters, the 420-yard dog-leg-left 10th. In many ways reminiscent of another C.B. Macdonald original, the Cape hole, number 10 enticed the player to bite off as much of the large lake as he dared with those successfully negotiating the longest carry facing the easiest second shot. Though modern equipment would render obsolete much of this strategy, the 10th was still a par-4 of great distinction and difficulty in its day.

The next such challenge came at number 13 where one faced perhaps the most instantly recognizable of all replica holes, the Biarritz. Modeled after a long-defunct clifftop par-3 in Biarritz, France, the Macdonald/Raynor/Banks versions were built exclusively in the 220-yard range and featured an almost geometrically-precise design. The large, squarish putting surface was always fronted by a four-to-six-foot deep swale, which in turn was fronted by a patch of fairway sometimes maintained as a part of the green. Long, narrow bunkers guarded both sides of this entire area, generally arranged in symmetrical pairs. Occasionally a smaller cross-bunker was situated well shy of the green, symbolic of the forced carry required on the across-the-chasm oceanfront original.

From the looks of it, Banks's Oneck Course rendition was the standard brute, measuring 220-yards and angled dead into the prevailing breeze. Interestingly, Westhampton was likely the only club ever to feature two Biarritzes, as Raynor himself had already built the 225-yard 17th on the club's 1915 layout, a fine hole which remains in play today.

The par-4 14th offered little respite as a 400-yarder continuing into the wind. A favoring breeze was regained at the 550-yard 15th, then lost once again at the two-shot 16th in preparation for a pair of difficult and memorable finishers.

The 160-yard 17th was based upon the famous Eden eleventh at St. Andrews, A fairly short one-shotter played to a green fronted by two bunkers and guarded long by water. On most replica versions, the rear hazard was approximated by a long, narrow bunker, though here at Westhampton, the further presence of Moriches Bay served to at least mirror the ambiance of the original.

The Oneck's finisher, however, went it one better, qualifying as a genuine classic. Running nearly at water's edge (separated only by the club's rather oddly-positioned entrance road), it was a full-blooded 430-yard par-4 whose drive was menaced by fairway traps right and a lake to the left. The approach then required as much finesse as power for the green complex was modeled after the famous Road 17th at St. Andrew's, a tremendously difficult target featuring a deep pot bunker front-left and a long, flanking trap (approximating the eponymous road) to the right and rear. Normally employed by Macdonald and Raynor on mid-length par-4s or moderately reachable par-5s, this long two-shot version seems more closely akin to the notoriously difficult original.

Sadly, the Oneck Course was among the shortest-lived of any topflight American facility, never enjoying even the opportunity to be polished up by the architect following an evaluation of early play. For one thing, Banks died less than two years after the course's genesis at the painfully young age of forty-eight. But even more significantly, the Oneck had the great misfortune of opening in eerie lockstep with the onset of the Depression, an economic albatross from which it could never escape. The course ceased being maintained in 1933 and remained an overgrown field for several years before ultimately being converted to luxury homesites. Meanwhile, just up the street, Raynor's original 1915 layout survives: an historic track of great character, but lacking the bold grandeur of Charles Banks's defunct classic.

How Westhampton Would Measure Up Today

Banks's intimately-crafted design offered a wonderful oceanfront setting, several first-rate holes and a consistently high level of challenge which, particularly in the wind, would still hold up nicely today. From a ratings-oriented perspective, however, we are presented with the age-old dilemma of length versus variety and character. There would, after all, have been very little room to stretch the Oneck much beyond its original 6,540-yard distance and as it already played to a par of 70, reclassifying a short par-5 or two likewise would not have been an option. Thus Westhampton's Oneck Course would best be classified with the Bel Airs, Creeks, and Apawamises of the world—classic designs worth seeing, even if they're a tad short in the age of titanium rocket launchers.

Often forgotten as one peruses the Macdonald/Raynor/Banks replica repertoire are the hallowed originals from which the architects drew their inspiration.

Among the par-3s, the most striking was likely the Biarritz, the third or "Chasm" hole at Biarritz, France. Gradually altered out of existence over the years, it began life at approximately 220 yards, the first 100-plus of which were a forced carry over a deep seaside gorge. It was, in its day, among the most difficult golf holes ever constructed.

North Berwick's ever-famous 193-yard Redan, shown on the previous page as it was surveyed in 1912, features the same green contouring (the putting surface falling away back-left) as its many replicas. Noteworthy, though, are the three seemingly superfluous short bunkers, and the fact that the front-left Redan bunker was, for many years, buttressed with a wall of wooden railroad sleepers as large as any ever erected by modern architects like Pete Dye.

St. Andrew's much-copied 172-yard Eden is really a hole more penal than strategic. Actually named "High (In)," it shares a large double green with hole number seven (whose path it actually crosses) and is fronted by a pair of scary bunkers, the 10-foot-deep Hill to the left and the pot-like Strath on the right. What makes the hole even more frightening is the presence of the Eden estuary long of the steeply contoured green, leaving the player few palatable options beyond hitting the putting surface—preferably below the pin.

Finally, the 130-yard Short was not a replica but a C.B. Macdonald original, its bunker-surrounded green contoured with the trademark horseshoe-shaped ridge. Debuting as the sixth hole of the National Golf Links of America, this initial version for some time also featured a front bunker buttressed by vertical wooden sleepers, placing Macdonald light years ahead of his time among fashion-conscious American architects.

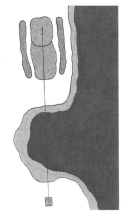

Third Hole at Biarritz, France.

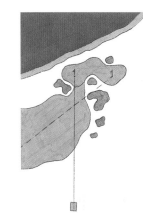

North Berwick's 193-yard Redan.

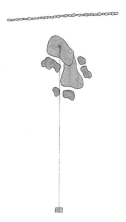

St. Andrew's 172-yard Eden.

St. Andrew's 172-yard Eden.

BILLY BELL & GEORGE C. THOMAS

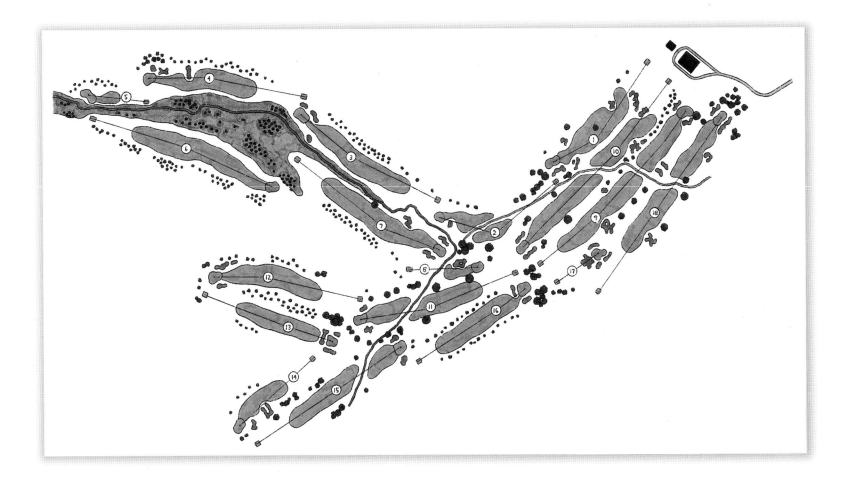

EL CABALLERO																				
355	347	400	394	144	482	430	175	516	3243	550	408	380	350	245	431	335	115	531	3345	6588
4	4	4	4	3	5	4	3	5	36	5	4	4	4	3	4	4	3	5	36	72

EL CABALLERO COUNTRY CLUB

TARZANA, CA

Opened in 1926 / 6,588 yards Par-72

Oddly contradictory to its wonderful weather and leisure-oriented lifestyle, the greater Los Angeles area is today one of America's worst when it comes to golf course availability. Surprising? Not to anyone who has driven east, often as far as Palm Springs, for a tee time or grazed like cattle through a six-hour round at venerable old Rancho Park. What might surprise such dedicated Angelinos, however, is the knowledge that once upon a time, their jaded, crowded, overfreewayed city was in fact a veritable golfer's paradise.

The 1931 edition of the American Annual Golf Guide listed no less than 46 regulation-sized facilities within Los Angeles County, a number constituting roughly 50% of the then-operating courses in the entire southern half of California. Perhaps even more impressive was the concentration of facilities along the city's West Side—that bastion of outrageously priced real estate running roughly from the Palos Verdes Peninsula in the South to the Santa Monica Mountains in the North. Within this now-teeming coastal expanse, a remarkable 28 regulation-sized golf courses once existed, fully 15 of which are no longer in play today.

While these long-lost layouts ranged in scope from rudimentary nine-holers in Santa Monica and Palms to ambitious 36-hole complexes at Fox Hills and Sunset Fields, there can be little doubt that the best of them—the facility offering the most in terms of variety, challenge, and thrilling golfing terrain—was also the most geographically removed: the El Caballero Country Club in Tarzana.

Not to be confused with the present-day club bearing the same name, the original El Caballero stood immediately adjacent to today's version, in the northern foothills of the Santa Monica Mountains. Carved from a small section of author Edgar Rice Burroughs's expansive ranch, it was intended to serve as the centerpiece for one of Southern California's earliest planned communities, named Tarzana in tribute to Burrough's most enduring character, Tarzan.

Contrary to popular belief, legendary architect George C. Thomas, Jr. was not the man chosen to build El Caballero, that honor going instead to his frequent construction supervisor Billy Bell. Thomas was a consultant in the course's design but articles detailing its opening made no mention of him, and in Thomas's classic volume *Golf Architecture in America*, he himself assigned Bell primary credit.

While it is unknown just how these two men came to meet, the positive influence which they exerted upon each other was obvious. In Bell's case, his own architectural career was off to a modest start prior to the collaboration and few would argue that the four courses upon which he consulted Thomas (El Caballero, Palos Verdes, and two courses at Northern California's

Hole number one, an outstanding strategic opener. (*Golf Illustrated*)

Castlewood) demonstrated a degree of sophistication generally absent from his truly solo work. Conversely, while Thomas is frequently noted for the wild, free-flowing style of his bunkering, a brief look at the hazards each man was building prior to joining forces clearly suggests that it was Bell who influenced Thomas in this regard and not vice versa.

Whatever the case, their teamwork certainly resulted in something special at El Caballero, a golf course which the great sportswriter Grantland Rice once rated among the very best on the entire West Coast. Key to the layout's excellence was the variety of its terrain, including a flat plain beneath the elevated clubhouse (broken in spots by a narrow drainage wash) and two hilly canyons, the larger of which was bisected by a wide, deep barranca. The architects utilized these options wonderfully, creating a course which, though lacking some of the bite inherent in Thomas's work at Riviera and Los Angeles Country Club, featured as much pure variety as either of those classic Golden Age designs.

El Caballero opened with a fine par-4 of 355 yards, its driving area divided by a single small tree, its green protected front-left by an especially deep bunker. The right side of the fairway offered the best angle of approach, a short iron to a fairly open target. But was one ready to aim for this bunker-and-rough-guarded side on the first real swing of the day? Following the shortish dogleg-right second, play moved westward up the canyon, first with a pair of solid par-4s, then with one of golf's most spectacular holes, the one-shot fifth.

In modern announcer-speak, this gorgeous 144-yarder would surely be called El Caballero's "Signature Hole," its slight body climbing into the uppermost reaches of the starkly beautiful canyon. Here the ever-dangerous barranca did more than lurk along the edges, instead cozying quite close to the left and rear of the L-shaped putting surface. Additionally, much of the green's right side was obscured by a large section of descending canyonside, thus requiring a shot either boldly aimed into this blind (but safer) area or laid dangerously close to the barranca-edged left. Great is the one-shotter that gives the player so much to consider as he stands upon the tee, but even greater is one situated in so spectacular a setting.

The 482-yard sixth began the trek back down the canyon, its descending terrain providing a

The unique and beautiful fifth, played directly into the top of the canyon.
(*The American Golfer*)

real chance to get home in two—or go for a big number if either shot strayed left toward the barranca. This same hazard then came into play one final time at number seven, a stout 430-yarder with a narrow green flanked on either side by sand.

After a brief respite at the 175-yard eighth, the course returned to the flat expanse beneath the clubhouse for the back-and-forth ninth and tenth, a pair of full-length par-5s which provided the better player with ample scoring opportunities. The exam quickly stiffened again at the 408-yard 11th, however, where one's approach had to be threaded between two large trees and carry the rather diluted remains of the barranca to reach an elevated, well-bunkered green.

Following the up-and-down canyon visit of holes 12 and 13, the 245-yard par-3 14th represented a favored ingredient of many Bell or Thomas designs: the immensely long one-shotter playing very nearly as a par-4. In this case a pair of imposing bunkers threatened pulled shots but a well-struck ball, presumably hit with a driver, figured to allow at least a fair chance of getting up and down for three.

El Caballero's finishers, running directly north toward the clubhouse, were a typically varied bunch, beginning with the 431-yard 15th where the final, dying tentacles of the barranca threatened the longest drives. Oddly, the 335-yard 16th was a somewhat undistinguished hole, offering little in the way of discernible strategy or challenge, save one's self-imposed pressure to make birdie at so crucial a juncture of play.

Bobby Cruickshank holing out at the 72nd green to win the 1927 Los Angeles Open.
(*Golf Illustrated*)

Thankfully, number 17 was another story. Frequently singled out by period writers for its all-or-nothing nature, it played anywhere from 95 to 115 yards to a small, severely contoured green all but surrounded by four large bunkers. The 18th, a pleasant three-shotter of 531 yards, then closed things out in somewhat more mellow fashion.

Though the course was very well thought of, successfully hosting the 1927 Los Angeles Open (won by Bobby Cruickshank), El Caballero eventually ran headlong into two perils common to the era. First came financial problems associated with the Depression, then a huge increase in the value of the club's land during America's post-World War II suburban expansion. Real estate developers were warded off for a time but ultimately Billy Bell's masterpiece was sold, its land eventually becoming one of the San Fernando Valley's more affluent residential neighborhoods.

How el Caballero Would Measure Up Today

As a cult favorite, with the canyon holes being calendar-shot regulars.

In a Southern California market short on genuine classics, the original El Caballero would garner a great deal of attention—but not serious comparisons to Riviera, the Valley Club of Montecito, or George Thomas's original layouts at Bel Air or Los Angeles Country Club on the region's very top shelf.

As mentioned previously, a noticeable stylistic difference existed between the handful of Billy Bell courses on which George Thomas consulted and those which Bell completed in a genuinely solo manner. Still, among Bell's 10 or so lost layouts, several Southern California efforts are worthy of note.

For aficionados, the most intriguing figures would be The Royal Palms Country Club, a long-lost 18-holer located in San Pedro, on the southwestern slopes of Los Angeles' Palos Verdes Peninsula. Having gained notoriety among the faithful with its singular appearance in George Thomas's famous volume *Golf Architecture in America* (the grainy old photo captioned simply, "General View, San Pedro Course, California"), The Royal Palms was a 6,334-yard, par-70 layout which meandered to and fro across the tops of stark, chaparral-covered hillsides high above the Pacific. Completed in 1925, it was not only Bell's most spectacular solo work but also one of his best. Remarkably, almost no documentation remains today regarding the specifics of its existence or the particulars of its demise.

Bell himself took particular pride in Midwick Country Club, a 6,309-yard facility located just south of what today is the 10 Freeway in Monterey Park, southeast of Pasadena. Originally designed by Scottish transplant Norman MacBeth, Midwick was substantially altered by Bell, becoming one of the first projects to show his trademark rough-edged bunker style. Featuring par-5s of 460 and 467 yards and two par-4s under 300, it was clearly not an overpowering layout. Yet its aesthetic qualities were such that its picture appeared in several of the architect's prominent period advertisements.

The famous photo of The Royal Palms—a spectacular Southern California mystery.
(*Golf Architecture in America*)

Perhaps Bell's most ambitious solo undertaking was the Sunset Fields Golf Club, a 36-hole complex located in what is today the Crenshaw district of west-central Los Angeles. Completed in 1927, both the 6,318-yard par-71 North and 6,555-yard par-72 South courses represented something slightly more inspired than your average big-city public fare, featuring a handful of replica holes and several stretches of open, sandy terrain. Like so many early L.A. facilities, Sunset Fields eventually bowed to Southern California's ever-escalating real estate values, with only a single neighborhood street, the rather anomalously named Fairway Drive, representing any hint of the neighborhood's golfing past.

CHARLES H. ALISON

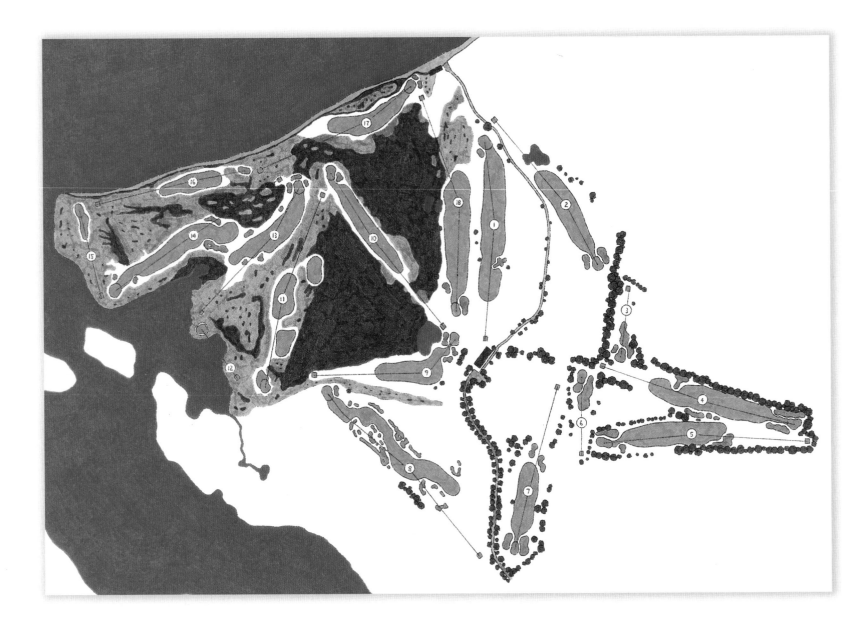

TIMBER POINT																				
450	420	160	470	485	180	380	520	370	3425	455	460	140	380	470	205	355	425	510	3400	6825
4	4	3	5	4	3	4	5	4	36	4	4	3	4	4	3	4	4	5	35	71

TIMBER POINT GOLF CLUB

GREAT RIVER, NY

Opened in 1925 / 6,825 yards Par-71

Among golf architecture's many noted design "teams," few have ever been more famous than the Golden Age pairing of H.S. Colt and C.H. Alison. Their partnership, begun when Alison joined Colt's already-established firm in or around 1908, would last for more than 40 years, frequently in conjunction with J.S.F. Morrison and the legendary Dr. Alister MacKenzie. Yet despite so obvious a business compatibility, Mssrs. Colt and Alison rarely if ever actually worked together, instead dividing the firm's workload into geographically defined zones and rigidly adhering to them. Colt handled jobs in Great Britain and Europe while Alison, ever the world traveler, took care of the firm's American, Japanese, South African, and Australian projects.

Though lacking the stateside design volume of Ross or Tillinghast, or the social entree of Macdonald and Raynor, the firm of Colt & Alison nevertheless drew several plum assignments in America with Alison, working solo, completing such gems as Sea Island, Milwaukee Country Club, and Knollwood in suburban Chicago. But perhaps the high esteem in which the firm was held was best illustrated by its selection in 1923 to design an ultra-private club to be located in an affluent section of Long Island's South Shore. It was called Timber Point.

The property, positioned upon a large promontory in the town of Great River, had previously served as the estate of a local millionaire, promptly being bought up by a group of his equally well-heeled neighbors upon the gentleman's passing. The group's plan was simple: to build a wealthy, extremely exclusive club offering only the best of facilities to its 100 carefully selected members. And while the oceanfront site undoubtedly showed tremendous potential as a golf course, the job undertaken by Charles Alison could hardly have been qualified as easy.

Inherent in Timber Point's development was the reclamation of over 100 acres of previously unusable land, some of it marsh, the rest retrieved from the very waters of Great South Bay. So ambitious a dredging operation took nearly two years to complete but left Alison with a property of almost unique variety, its upper reaches offering dense pine forest and gently rolling terrain, its lower half encompassing sandy dunes and ocean frontage. Not surprisingly, he utilized such a landscape to create a storybook layout, one which must surely have qualified as his personal masterpiece. Its variety was textbook, its strategic and scenic qualities above reproach. And Timber Point was also difficult—"*extremely* difficult"—measuring an enormous 6,825 yards from the championship tees. Alternately a mix of Pine Valley and Kiawah Island, it was, quite simply, spectacular.

The course began in character with a long and difficult par-4, a 450-yarder played southward toward the water, dead into the prevailing wind. This breeze then worked in the player's favor as the routing turned inland at the 420-yard second, another solid two-shotter whose green was flanked by the sort of large, roundish bunkers typical of a mid-'20s Alison design.

Fairway view of number six, an inland hole likened to Pine Valley. (*Golf Illustrated*)

Perhaps the largest maintained bunker on the course was in play at the 160-yard third, a wandering, rather modern-looking hazard fronting a small, pear-shaped green. It was here that Timber Point began its five-hole venture into the forest, a pleasant stretch which drew the aforementioned comparisons to Pine Valley but which, in reality, more closely resembled British heathland courses such as Walton Heath or Sunningdale.

One's first real birdie opportunity came at the fourth, a 470-yard par-5, made easier by a mostly helping breeze. Following a demanding tee shot between large fairway bunkers, the player was faced with the prospect of a long-iron or wooden second played to a relatively deep putting surface. More easily reached in two than several of Timber Point's par-4s and lacking much of a layup area, this unique hole likely encouraged going for the green as much as any par-5 ever built.

Oddly, the fifth, measuring a full 15 yards longer, was played as a par-4, indicating Alison's penchant for the occasional par-stretching two-shotter. Routed back into the breeze, its difficulty was even further enhanced by a green angled right, behind another immense sand hazard.

Following the difficult one-shot sixth and straight-ahead seventh, the layout emerged from the woods onto sandy terrain even more reminiscent of the British heathlands. The 510-yard par-5 eighth negotiated this land smartly, its flanks marked by numerous bunkers and waste areas, its into-the-wind distance of a distinctly three-shot nature. The 370-yard dogleg-left ninth then provided one final rest before the difficulty factor was stepped up exponentially.

There can be little doubt that it was Timber Point's back nine which served as the course's most significant draw, its oceanfront, wind-buffeted routing being among the most difficult, intimidating, and breathtaking ever constructed.

It commenced with the 455-yard 10th, a gargantuan, into-the-wind par-4 running directly across the filled-in marshland. Difficult enough in its own right, this brute (which surely killed the temptation of any impatient members to "sneak off the back nine") really only served as a warmup for the awesome 460-yard 11th, a hole whose design lineage was almost as impressive as its massive challenge.

Popularly known as Three Island (though rather curiously listed on early scorecards as Sahara), it was based upon Dr. Alister MacKenzie's hypothetical layout of an optimum two-shotter which captured a 1914 design contest sponsored by the British magazine *Country Life*. Providing three distinct lines of play with starkly different levels of risk and reward, MacKenzie's prize-winning drawing was utilized, with some alteration, by Charles Blair Macdonald as the 18th hole of his legendary course at Lido Beach, New York. Here at Timber Point, a full eight years after the Lido's construction, Alison too paid tribute to MacKenzie's conceptual creation, resulting in a long par-4 with multiple driving options and a green virtually surrounded by rugged, unmaintained dunesland. A curious quirk: by the time of Timber Point's construction, MacKenzie had parted company with Colt & Alison, a breakup which, according to prevalent thought, was not altogether amicable. Thus the motivation and timing of Alison's replica must be considered at least somewhat mysterious.

11th green in the foreground, the par-5 eighth in the distance. (*Golf Illustrated*)

The 12th—all 140 yards of it—might well have been the layout's most memorable hole, its short-iron approach playing across a corner of the club's yacht basin to an elevated green completely surrounded by sand. An all-or-nothing test in the most exciting style, this was easily the club's shortest hole and, with an elevated tee looking out over the back nine and Great South Bay, possibly its most beautiful.

Timber Point's finishers were a long and dangerous bunch, venturing across wide-open sand and marshland, and down to the very edges of the ocean. The 14th, yet another back-breaking two-shotter at 470 yards, was especially difficult, featuring a tee shot that had to be threaded left-to-right between two carefully angled bunkers. Only partially aided by the prevailing wind, the player was then faced with a long iron or wood to another small green set off by itself amid the now-familiar sand-covered landscape. Interestingly, Alison borrowed this design from his own portfolio, having built a strikingly similar hole (since altered into unrecognizable homogeneity) two years earlier on the 14th at Knollwood. He would later duplicate it at the Milwaukee Country Club as well.

Like the 11th, Timber Point's 205-yard 15th also was something of a MacKenzie replica, based upon his famous Gibraltar hole at Moortown, England. Playing directly into the teeth of the wind, it too required a tremendously long approach, its large, sand-encircled green elevated beautifully against the brilliant ocean backdrop.

Returning westward, numbers 16 and 17 were the club's only true seaside holes, a par of par-4s measuring 355 and 425 yards, respectively. Pressed snugly against a narrow, remote stretch of seashore, the shorter 16th required a drive positioned between beach and fairway bunker, then a particularly precise approach to a green ringed, not unlike a doughnut, by wild, open sand. The drive at 17 was only slightly more forgiving, while its approach, this time played through a crosswind with a mid-iron, was similarly fraught with danger.

Following so rough a stretch, the downwind 510-yard 18th might almost have seemed a respite, but its problems (and options) were many. The tee shot was typically demanding, requiring a 180-yard carry over marshland, but it also allowed the more aggressive player to gain an advantage by biting off a bit more of the dogleg corner. From here one could have a go at the putting surface or lay back safely, the optimum right-side layup area guarded by another well-positioned bunker just to keep things interesting.

With such wide-ranging media coverage during golf's 1920s popularity boom, how did a course as great as Timber Point receive such little notoriety? Because, as with many ultra-exclusive clubs, it shunned the limelight thoroughly, discouraging outside play and refusing to host any events of more than local prominence. Its exclusivity, in fact, was such that upon being asked for a donation to help local authorities combat the area's annual mosquito menace, the membership refused, preferring the mosquitoes to the larger crowds which they feared might descend upon the area were it known to be pest-free. Similarly, when the owner of a neighboring 1,500-acre estate passed away, the club purchased the property (which today comprises Heckscher State Park) as insulation against an ever-encroaching world.

Of course, as with many similarly-minded clubs, such exclusivity drastically limited the potential new membership pool, inevitably resulting in long-term economic hardship. Though Timber Point did manage to weather the Depression, its fortunes sagged irreversibly during World War II, causing its eventual sale to Suffolk County for use as a municipal facility. Reconfigured to 27 holes in 1972, remnants of the original layout remain scattered among the three nines, but they bear only passing resemblance to the beauty, grandeur, and remarkable challenge of C.H. Alison's unforgettable original.

The tiny 12th, a pitch across a corner of the yacht basin. 14th fairway and 15th green visible in the distance. (*Golf Illustrated*)

The Gibraltar fifteenth: 200 yards, dead into the wind, water long, sand everywhere else. (*Golf Illustrated*)

How Timber Point Would Measure Up Today

That room existed in many places to lengthen Timber Point is almost irrelevant since several of its best holes were already pushing today's USGA yardage limits in 1923! With its tremendous challenge, variety, and ambiance, this golf course would unquestionably still hold a position among anyone's very best. Throw in the added boost provided by its age and tradition and, for the numerically oriented, a top 15-25 ranking seems about right.

DEVEREUX EMMET

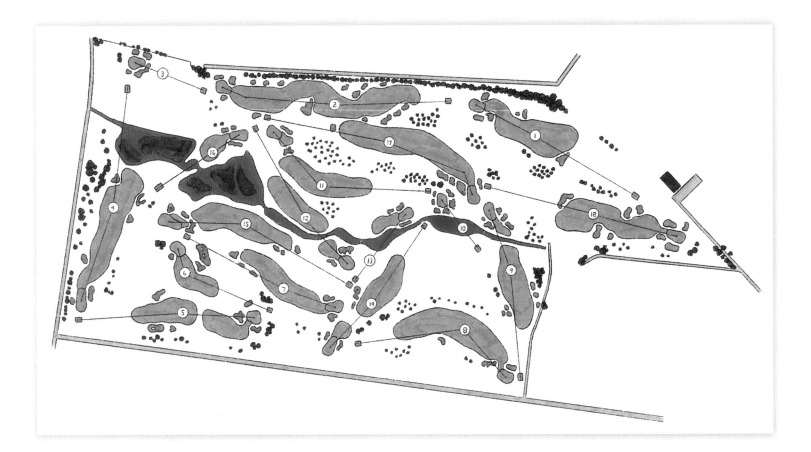

MEADOWBROOK HUNT																				
400	535	160	470	410	260	375	405	390	3405	140	410	375	190	290	440	220	470	420	2955	6360
4	5	3	5	4	4	4	4	4	37	3	4	4	3	4	4	3	5	4	34	71

MEADOWBROOK HUNT CLUB
WESTBURY, NY

Opened in 1916 / 6,360 yards Par-71

By any reasonable definition, the title "Father of American Golf Course Architecture" must be bestowed upon Mr. Charles Blair Macdonald, player, organizer, designer, and pontificator supreme. This can safely be said because while many a talented architect operated in this country during the teens and 1920s, all clearly were followers of Macdonald and his medium-altering masterpiece at The National Golf Links of America. True, a rare notable such as Walter Travis or Donald Ross was practicing course design earlier, but Travis (U.S. Amateur champion in 1900, '01, and '03, British Amateur champion in '04) was balancing this work against an active playing career while Ross surely did not hit the creative stride that would make him famous until the mid-teens.

Yet often forgotten amid the dizzying array of post-Macdonald talent was one man of real ability who was a genuine contemporary of C.B.'s: Devereux Emmet.

Emmet, born in 1861, was only five years younger than Macdonald and similarly graced with connections to monied society. A native of New York City, he enjoyed the leisurely life of a sportsman, generally scheduling his existence around an annual cycle of raising hunting dogs. Purchasing the animals down South each spring, he would spend the summer training them on his Long Island estate, sell them in Ireland each autumn, then spend a good part of the winter months playing golf in the British Isles and, in later life, the Bahamas. A fine player, he competed frequently and for a good many years, actually winning the 1928 Bahamas Amateur at the ripe old age of 66.

Though Emmet would later reflect back upon a lack of preparedness for the task, he received his first architectural job in 1897, building the nine-hole Island Golf Links in Garden City, New York. The Island Links was a popular affair and a year later Emmet expanded it into the 18-hole Garden City Golf Club that remains (with mounds and bunkering added by Walter Travis) the classically enduring layout that we know today.

Despite the obvious prestige associated with Garden City, Emmet's design career initially proceeded slowly, seldom including more than one course per year and generally not involving payment for services rendered. Happy with his rich-man's lifestyle, he instead became one of Macdonald's charter members at The National, also contributing directly to its creation by bringing back from Britain reports on many of the classic holes that C.B. would soon be emulating.

But the design bug would catch up with Emmet, resulting in a body of work which eventually exceeded 75 courses. Geographically his practice ranged from Connecticut as far south as North Carolina and the Bahamas but, in fact, its true focus was the New York metropolitan area. Regrettably, more than one-half of his courses are no longer in existence, many of which were among his best. And near the top of that list was the Meadowbrook Hunt Club.

Contrary to its name, polo was actually the dominant early pastime at Meadowbrook and much of the club's enduring fame comes from its initial involvement in equestrian sport. The membership was, however, treated to an 1887 golfing exhibition by British Amateur champion Horace Hutchinson and, despite a lukewarm response, eventually began play on a nine-hole facility in 1894. Lack of interest led to the abandonment of that site 11 years later but by 1916 the club's golfing element, tired of interloping at nearby Piping Rock and Nassau Country Club, managed to once again carry the day. Emmet was hired to build them 18 holes on an estate across the road from their original site and while this course would later be altered (reportedly by A.W. Tillinghast), its general routing seems to have been fairly well maintained. The layout is presented here as it appeared in 1940.

It opened with a pair of man-sized holes measuring 400 and 535 yards, the latter a very fine par-5 running southward along the property's boundary with neighboring Mitchell Airfield.

Following a mid-length par-3 came a second par-5, the very tempting 470-yard fourth. Here the player's drive had to cross the widest expanse of Meadow Brook and, if aimed aggressively, a single right-side fairway bunker as well. Doing so successfully would open up a straight-on angle for a long-iron approach, whereas a tee shot played further left brought a large left-hand greenside bunker very much into play. This same challenge remained even for a laid-up second with the more desirable right side guarded by a single fairway bunker some 90 yards shy of the green.

The sixth was a similarly thought-provoking hole, a tiny two-shotter of 260 yards. Once again Emmet set his angles wonderfully, offering either a safe drive-and-pitch route or a shorter direct line toward the flag. The latter, naturally, required a sizable carry over lots of sand, often intimidating the faint-of-heart down the open left side. The catch: a ball played too

Sam Snead tees off during the 1953 Goodall Round Robin tournament. He would win the event in the two years to follow. (R.W. Miller Golf Library)

far left brought a small greenside bunker into play, requiring that most difficult of shots, the quickly-stopping three-quarter pitch.

A bit of mystery surrounds the 140-yard 10th, a hole which by some reports originally played slightly shorter and to an island green. Though World War II-era aerials clearly show no such animal, the island green was in fact a favored ploy of Emmet, making the concept of its earlier existence a viable one. By wartime, however, the hole had evolved into an across-the-water shot to a green largely surrounded by five rather artistic bunkers.

Meadow Brook itself returned to play at the 375-yard 12th, and considerably more so at the dangerous 190-yard 13th. It also guarded the right side of the 440-yard 15th, the club's longest par-4 played over a pair of crossbunkers to an exceptionally large putting surface.

The brook scarcely came into play on the three finishing holes, though they still represented an interesting mix of challenge and opportunity. The 220-yard 16th crossed the water for the final time and, with three bunkers guarding its narrow green, was a place where par was always welcome. Number 17, on the other hand, was a distinctly reachable 470-yard par-5, the last 100 yards of which were dominated by a series of right-side bunkers waiting to swallow a mishit second. The 18th, a 420-yarder, closed things out with a flourish of difficulty, its nine bunkers mandating power and accuracy on both drive and approach.

Though hardly as tournament-famous as several of its Long Island neighbors, Meadowbrook did host significant events in its twilight years, with its Goodall Round Robin won by Dr. Cary Middlecoff in 1953 and Sam Snead in '54 and '55. By this time, however, New York State had officially condemned the property to make room for the new Meadowbrook Parkway, a road which became a reality in the middle of the decade. Thus forcibly evicted, the Meadowbrook membership left their golf course and adjacent polo fields, purchased land in nearby Jericho and hired Dick Wilson to build them the longer, distinctly more modern track which they continue to play today.

Is it any wonder that golf eclipsed equestrian pursuits among America's leading sportsmen? (*The American Golfer*)

How Meadowbrook Would Measure Up Today

Given the relative congestion of its interior holes, Meadowbrook might have run into logistical problems with higher volumes of play and modern equipment. Ample room existed to lengthen some of the perimeter holes (especially the wonderful fourth) but in general, the tightness of the property would have limited its potential to grow into the modern era. Still, in its 1940 configuration, Meadowbrook would be a lot of fun to play—and, after Garden City, quite possibly the best remaining Emmet design in the New York metropolitan area.

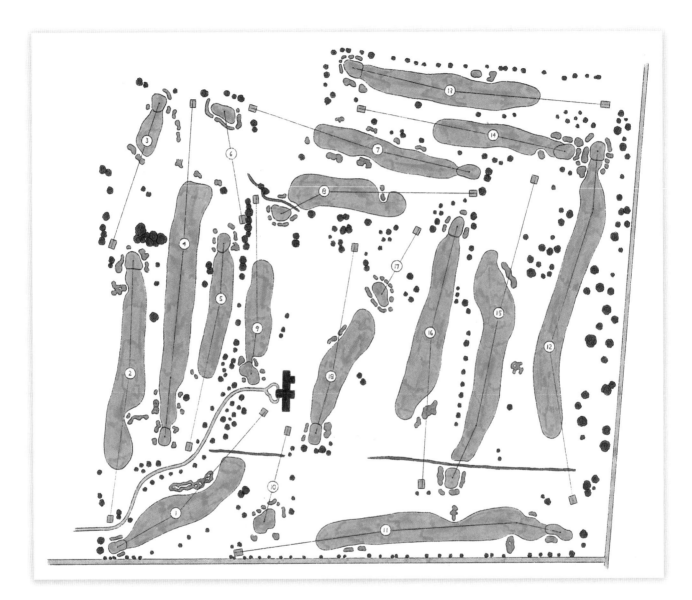

POMONOK																				
325	418	235	521	320	170	375	325	275	2964	153	508	575	413	330	476	410	108	300	3273	6237
4	4	3	5	4	3	4	4	4	35	3	5	5	4	4	5	4	3	4	37	72

POMONOK COUNTRY CLUB

FLUSHING, NY

Opened in 1921 / 6,237 yards Par-72

When the subject of golf's greatest architects comes up for discussion, Devereux Emmet's name is seldom among the first to be mentioned. This second-rate status may in some ways be justified, for the overall quality of his work, even in so subjective a medium, cannot be held on par with the Tillinghasts, MacKenzies, and Macdonalds of the field. Yet the volume of his practice was considerable, his client list impressive, and his portfolio at the very least notable, if not a little bit more.

One reason for Emmet's relative anonymity may be the loss of so many courses to post-World War II suburban expansion. Another may be that among those facilities still remaining, relatively tight tracts of urban and suburban land have severely limited clubs' abilities to expand their layouts in step with modern equipment. As an example, a brief perusal of 10 remaining Emmet facilities in the New York metropolitan area reveals an average championship-tee length of 6,364 yards, far less than many higher-profile area courses which began life no longer but have since grown enormously.

Yet while Emmet's existing layouts may run shorter, they tend to offer something patently lacking in longer modern courses: variety.

Indeed, while Emmet was well-established long before such trendsetters as Dr. Alister MacKenzie and George Thomas highlighted that elusive commodity atop their written commandments on sound design, he practiced it comprehensively. Just a brief look at almost any Emmet layout

off to developers in 1949.

How Pomonok Would Measure Up Today

As a member of a not-so-exclusive club: "Ex-PGA Championship Sites That No One Remembers." It's not that Pomonok wasn't a good golf course, for obviously it was. But it definitely was not Emmet's best, nor was it a particular standout in New York's thoroughly-rich world of pre-Depression golf design. Several holes would still thrill even today but on balance, do the names Keller, Llanerch, and Columbine Country Clubs ring any bells?

With just over half of his estimated 79 career designs either gone or built over beyond recognition, the pound-for-pound champion of lost courses must be Devereux Emmet. The primary reason for this is, as any realtor knows, location, location, location. For while Emmet's entree into New York society yielded many a choice project, a high percentage of these were located very close to or within the nation's largest city, making them an endangered species when it came time for the Big Apple to become huge.

Among the best of these lost New York-area facilities was the West Course of the Huntington Crescent Club, one of two 18-holers built for the club by Emmet and his occasional partner, A.H. Tull, upon the former Roy Rainey estate. Stretching to a then-very long 6,740 yards, the West was the club's championship layout and featured a pair of excellent par-3s, the 215-yard 10th (which required a 185-yard carry across a 100-foot-deep ravine) and the tiny 122-yard eighth. Designed to be an all-around sportsman's paradise, the Crescent Club's development was scuttled by the Depression, though several of the West Course's original holes remain in play on the back nine of the club's present-day 18.

Huntington Crescent West's 122-yard eighth, a typically-dangerous short Emmet par-3. (*Golf Illustrated*)

Equally notable—in terms of its pedigree, if nothing else—was the Rockwood Hall Country Club. A 1926 Emmet/Tull collaboration, Rockwood Hall was built upon the Tarrytown estate of the deceased William Rockefeller, a marvelously scenic 400-acre plot situated directly above the waters of the Hudson River. Whether Mr. Rockefeller endorsed this posthumous usage of his beloved country home is not a matter of record but regardless, the original layout measuring 6,206 yards was considered among the region's most scenic and enjoyable tests. It also featured a healthy dose of the standard Emmet variety, offering par-3s ranging from 136 to 220 yards, par-4s from 275 to 447 and par-5s from 463 to 600! With the club plagued by financial problems right from the start, plans for a second 18 never got off the ground, though the original was altered substantially by A.W. Tillinghast in 1929. A victim of the Depression, Rockwood Hall closed its doors for good in 1939.

Almost equally short-lived was the Grassy Sprain Country Club in nearby Bronxville, a 6,512-yard, par-73 facility located on either side of today's Central Avenue, just south of Tuckahoe Road. A hilly, wooded and very attractive layout, Grassy Sprain catered to a colorful crowd that included legendary hustler Titanic Thompson. It was also the site of the 1925 Metropolitan Open, a then highly prestigious event won by Gene Sarazen.

Rockwood Hall's 140-yard all-carry 11th. (*The American Golfer*)

Emmet's habit of including one extremely difficult par-3 may have reached its zenith here at the 245-yard 12th, a behemoth played sharply downhill past a pair of large elm trees to a green guarded left by Sprain Brook. Frequently losing members to the Westchester area's more established clubs since its inception, Grassy Sprain was sold to developers in 1938.

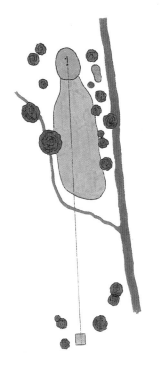

The 245-yard 12th at Grassy Sprain, the 'Robber's Roost.' Played from a tee elevated high above the fairway through a narrow corridor of trees.

Another lost Emmet hole of note was the third at Old Westbury Golf Club in Garden City, a 475-yard par-5 that offered a safe, roundabout path to the green or a more dangerous, bunker-carrying two-shot route. The course itself was one of the architect's most demanding, its 6,455 yards playing to a par of 71. Here too was the requisite Emmet variety, with par-4s ranging from the backbreaking 460-yard opener to the 315-yard 12th, and the obligatory monster par-3 at the 250-yard ninth. Located on wide-open land where the old Long Island Motor Parkway crossed Clinton Road, the Old Westbury site today houses the Roosevelt Field Shopping Center and a section of the Meadowbrook Parkway.

Emmet also served as architect for one of the most ambitious golf projects ever undertaken at the Salisbury Country Club in East Meadow where, between 1917 and 1925, he laid out five regulation 18-hole courses for resort developer J.J. Lannin. Of the five, only the showpiece Number Four, site of Walter Hagen's then-record fourth PGA Championship in 1926, survives as part of Nassau County's present-day Eisenhower Park.

Among the defunct, Number Three was likely the strongest, initially measuring 6,447 yards before being lengthened to 6,585 yards in the mid-1920s. It also shared a rather daunting oddity with the 6,215-yard Number Two course: 600-yard par-5 finishers to bring the player home in grand-but-exhausting style. The Number One course was also notable for its par-5s, specifically for packing four of them into its 3,288-yard outward half. Measuring 6,273 yards overall, it played to a par of 73, offering three sub-300-yard two-shotters to offset all

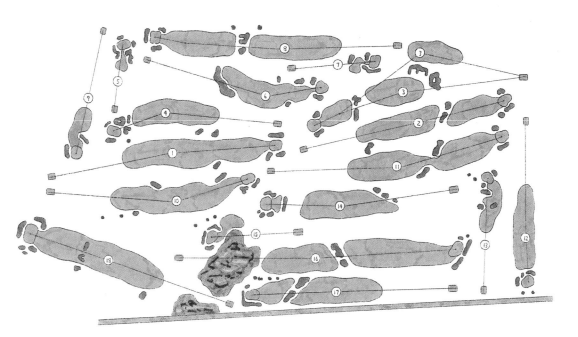

Emmet's rolling, treeless Old Westbury design.

OLD WESTBURY																				
460	435	475	345	130	335	180	490	250	3100	400	485	315	210	410	155	545	400	435	3355	6455
4	4	5	4	3	4	3	5	3	35	4	5	4	3	4	3	5	4	4	36	71

of that early length. Finally, the Number Five course stretched to 6,526 yards and the uncommon par of 74, making it perhaps the easiest of the quintuplet upon which to post a good score. Like so many clubs of the era, Salisbury ran into financial trouble during the Depression, beginning a gradual evolution into today's Trent Jones-influenced Eisenhower Park.

One final course indicative of Emmet's New York City work was the 1923 Queens Valley Golf Club, a fine layout in most locales but largely overlooked in this then-elite golfing neighborhood. Measuring 6,305 yards, it played to a par of 73 and featured six par-5s, the most noteworthy being the 548-yard 18th with its three crossbunkers and a small pond threatening one's second shot. The usually modest Emmet himself wrote quite favorably of Queens Valley, believing that "several very fine drive and pitch holes" and the long dogleg-right eighth, combined with a wonderfully convenient location, made it "the most desirable club near New York."

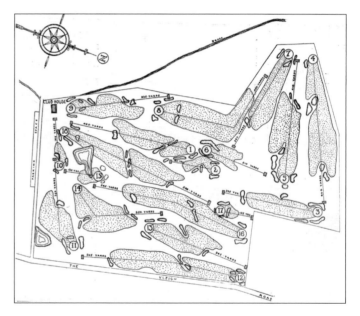

Queens Valley GC, a fine layout overshadowed
by some high-powered golfing neighbors.
(*Golf Illustrated*)

WILLIAM FLYNN

BOCA RATON (South)																				
330	200	420	385	460	330	410	195	555	3285	405	395	205	490	135	320	385	570	410	3315	6600
4	3	4	4	5	4	4	3	5	36	4	4	3	5	3	4	4	5	4	36	72

BOCA RATON RESORT & CLUB
BOCA RATON, FL

South course, 1928/ +/- 6,600 yards Par-72

The development of the state of Florida in general, and its famous Gold Coast in particular, has always made for interesting reading; its background of palm trees, tropical breezes, fabulous wealth, and strange characters often resembling a cross between F. Scott Fitzgerald's *The Great Gatsby* and a Damon Runyon short story.

Weather and leisure-oriented lifestyle considered, the game of golf has long been an integral part of that development. In most locales, it dates back to a point shortly after the arrival of Henry Flagler's Florida East Coast rail line, which laid its track from St. Augustine to Miami between 1893 and 1896. With Flagler's trains came hostelries in which to house his guests and with these hostelries, at least in the cities of St. Augustine, Ormond Beach, Palm Beach, and Miami, came golf. Primitive golf really, played over rudimentary layouts with rudimentary equipment, but golf nonetheless.

It would not be long, however, before Florida's lustrous prospects made the serious development of the game a reality. By 1920, architects-to-the-stars like Donald Ross, A.W. Tillinghast, and Seth Raynor had all built significant courses in the Sunshine State. By the time the mid-1920s land boom arrived, Florida had become one of the hotbeds of golf's growth nationwide.

Among Henry Flagler's early developments, Palm Beach and Miami would enjoy the brightest futures, with Palm Beach in particular becoming as synonymous as any American address with wealth, exclusivity, and prestige. A good deal of this image was the product of a unique, semi-Spanish style of architecture made popular in the area by free-spirited designer Addison

Mizner. The intrepid Mr. Mizner proved something of a visionary—and an adventurer, a wit, and, in all likelihood, a bit of a lunatic as well. Not satisfied with simply altering forever the horizon of the flattest state in the Union, he set about in 1925 to build his dream city, a luxurious coastal enclave located some 20 miles south of Palm Beach that he named Boca Raton.

Forming the Mizner Development Company, he began by auctioning off real estate, his first six weeks of sales totaling a staggering $26 million. Shortly thereafter he built the 100-room Cloister Inn, a $1.25 million pleasure palace which remains today as a focal point of the entire Boca area. Naturally, with its 1926 opening attracting only the most desired clientele, an appropriate level of amenities was required. Thus came such offbeat additions as El Camino Real, a stupendously wide entry road bisected by a gondola-filled canal, as well as standards like tennis, polo, an airfield and, of course, golf.

Though the presence of Donald Ross to design a never-built course for the nearby Ritz-Carlton hotel somewhat muddies the historical picture, Philadelphia-based architect William Flynn (along with his construction partner Howard Toomey) was the architect responsible for the development of Mizner's 36 holes. Oddly, he and Ross met on site and were actually photographed together, but there is ample evidence to suggest that Toomey and Flynn alone planned what would eventually become the club's North and South courses. The somewhat overlooked North turned out slightly shorter than its sister layout but played over the same wild, sand-strewn landscape. A wonderful "second" course, it measured roughly 6,500 yards and was a good, solid test of golf.

The South Course, however, was a keeper.

The famous Cloister Inn under construction, circa 1925. Several holes from the since-altered North Course are visible beyond. (Boca Raton Historical Society)

Located to the south of El Camino Real and running parallel (but not immediately adjacent) to the Intracoastal Waterway, it was a roughly 6,600-yard, par-72 test that was widely considered among the very best in the nation. Laid out across more of Florida's flat, sandy terrain, it featured an impressive four selections in a series of 1934 articles in *The American Golfer* highlighting the country's greatest holes. The series' author, Grantland Rice, was one of the club's obvious fans, likening several of its challenges to Pine Valley and writing in 1930 that "Toomey and Flynn have handled more than one fine golf production, but nothing to surpass the work they have done here." With Flynn having already completed Cherry Hills, Virginia's Cascades, and virtually all of his classic Philadelphia-area designs (Shinnecock Hills would come a year later), this was no small praise indeed.

Surprisingly, precious little documentation exists regarding the precise yardages of the South Course; thus the numbers presented herein (scaled from aerial photographs and the handful of distances reported in *The American Golfer*) are approximate but relatively accurate.

The layout opened simply enough with a nondescript 330-yard par-4, though the 200-yard second likely served as an abrupt wakeup call. The first really fine test, however, came at the 420-yard third, a dogleg-right requiring a drive slightly faded over a very Shinnecock Hills-like sea of bunkering. The fourth, stretching nearly 400 yards, was similarly challenging, establishing fully this strategic (and copious) bunkering style.

The fifth was a curious hole, apparently measuring little more than 460 yards, yet almost certainly a three-shotter considering the overall par of 72. Of course, it was also the South Course's only hole routed directly into the incoming sea breeze, and a long, angled bunker short-right of the green dictated choosing between a carefully measured layup or boldly attempting to reach it in two.

The sixth was a 330-yard drive-and-pitch rated among the best of its type by the club's leg-
endary pro Tommy Armour. The preferred left side of the fairway flanked by four huge bunkers, it was a slight dogleg right requiring a delicate approach to a shallow green tucked behind three more substantial sand hazards.

Following the 410-yard seventh and short eighth, the outward half closed with the frequently honored ninth, a massive par-5 stretching roughly 555 yards. Clearly a legitimate three-shotter, it utilized a good deal more of Flynn's waste-area-like bunkering and was a rarity for holes of such length in that none of the three shots allowed one simply to flail aimlessly away.

Perhaps the South Course's best opportunity for scoring came at holes 13 through 15, a group measuring roughly 490, 135 and 320 yards, respectively. The 13th was a second reachable par-5, whose small green was fronted by one perfectly positioned bunker, once again requiring as much finesse as power. The tiny 14th was a beauty, played across several grass-dotted bunkers to an appropriately small putting surface. The drive-and-pitch 15th, meanwhile, likely presented the course's tightest driving target.

Following one more mid-length par-4 came the 570-yard 17th, something of a replica of the famous "Hell's Half Acre" seventh at Pine Valley, a course with which Flynn had been closely associated since its inception. The primary challenge here, as on the vaunted original, was an enormous fairway-wide waste area occupying nearly 100 yards of prime second-shot landing space, requiring either two robust swings or, having laid up, an inordinately-long third. The 18th, a 410-yard par-4, likely seemed a breather by comparison.

Though golf holes comprising part of a newer development do occupy por-
tions of the land, Boca Raton's South Course is long removed from the South Florida landscape. It can be remembered as both a great test of golf and an outstandingly natural one, its layout shaped into the open, sandy flow of the terrain and featuring none of the mundane designer's best Florida friend, the artificial lake. The club also represented a great part of golfing history, serving as the winter home of Tommy Armour and, later, Sam Snead. Armour, who spent long hours seated beneath his umbrella instructing one affluent duffer after another, was so enamored of the place that he pictured it on the cover of his bestselling 1953 book *How to Play Your Best Golf All the Time.*

A rare photo of William Flynn and Donald Ross, posed (pleasantly) during their concurrent work at Boca Raton. (Boca Raton Historical Society)

Though the Boca Raton resort remains one of the world's finest, the demise of its South Course represents a great loss to a region where 99 layouts in 100 look alike and genuine classics are few and very far between. But forget South Florida. Fans of classic architecture everywhere should mourn this absence for after Shinnecock Hills, the South Course at Boca Raton may well have been William Flynn's finest overall design.

How Boca Raton Would Measure Up Today

The 135-yard 14th: all carry and typical of the sandy South Florida terrain.
(*The American Golfer*)

As a second great golf course for South Florida.

Lacking a pair of coastal dune ridges and several hundred yards of ocean frontage, the South Course would not be another Seminole. But with its plethora of standout holes, marvelous bunkering, and ever-present sea breezes, comparisons to Shinnecock Hills (albeit a distinctly flatter Florida version) are not without some merit.

In short, a surefire fixture in most Top 100s.

Looking toward the 17th green from the midst of Hell's Half Acre—not a place in which to enjoy one's Florida vacation.
(*The American Golfer*)

54

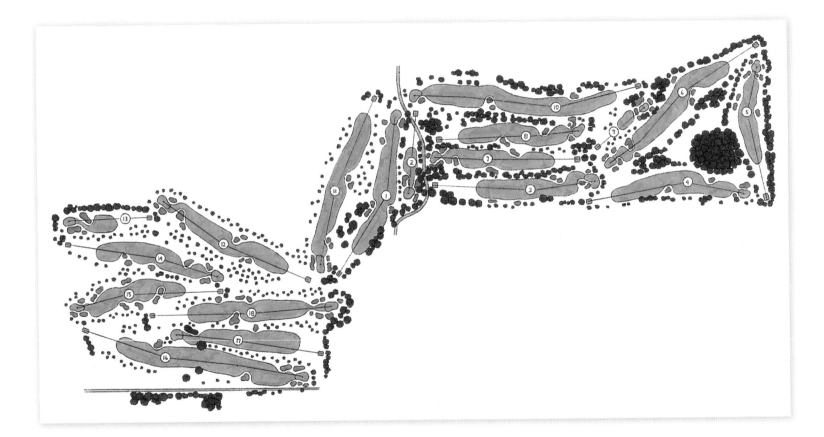

MILL ROAD FARM																				
435	200	410	405	340	485	370	365	160	3170	580	435	420	210	390	375	570	385	465	3830	7000
4	3	4	4	4	5	4	4	3	35	5	4	4	3	4	4	5	4	4	37	72

MILL ROAD FARM GOLF CLUB

LAKE FOREST, IL

Opened in 1926 / +/- 7,000 yards Par-72

Though America has enjoyed many periods of great economic prosperity, perhaps no single era remains as memorable—as indicative of the quintessential images of American wealth and consumption—as the Roaring Twenties. During this time of unprecedented economic expansion the phrase "the good life" took on new meaning, with recreational sports such as golf, tennis, and polo enjoying previously unheard of levels of growth.

Imbued with a desire to enjoy the leisurely lifestyle made possible by a booming and supposedly infallible economy, many of America's wealthiest citizens began constructing luxurious private estates, both in the suburban countrysides of their home cities and in more traditional resort locales like Newport and the Hamptons. Perhaps out of genuine love for the game, perhaps out of ego, such estates frequently included a private golf course, an amenity which, among the very affluent, became more or less *de rigueur* for the times.

Naturally, high society was interested in having only the best, making it inevitable that nearly every important golf architect of the period become involved in at least some estate course construction. With an average full-size layout consuming roughly 150 acres, however, these projects frequently faced logistical restrictions, and as a result varied greatly in their size and scope. Charles Blair Macdonald, for example, utilized a unique configuration of three classic green complexes (a Redan, a Short, and an Eden) and carefully placed tee boxes to create a "nine-hole" layout on only 25 acres for his friend Payne Whitney's Manhasset, New York, estate. On the West Coast meanwhile, Dr. Alister MacKenzie is credited with building a pair of nine-hole par-3 courses for actors Harold Lloyd and Charlie Chaplin on their Beverly Hills properties.

Given the many components involved, it is interesting to note that the finest estate course ever built was designed not by the well-connected Macdonald or MacKenzie but by Philadelphia-based William Flynn. Nor was it located among the bastions of old, traditional Eastern wealth but in the equally affluent (though somewhat less coastal) town of Lake Forest, Illinois.

The Mill Road Farm Golf Club, one of the least-documented and most mysterious courses of all time, was the brainchild of Chicago advertising executive Albert Lasker. A man blessed with great imagination and ambition, Lasker was the epitome of the self-made, "up by the bootstraps" American. Beginning at the very bottom, he revitalized the advertising game (inventing, among other things, the radio commercial) and eventually took over the firm for which he worked, the industry giant known today as Foote, Cone & Belding.

Lasker's Lake Forest estate was built on the opulent scale that one might expect from such a success story, occupying 480 acres and costing approximately $3.5 million to construct. It included a movie theater, a pool, stables, tennis courts, and an extensive complex of greenhouses and gardens, the latter being used to experiment with various types of grasses in advance of the property's prized centerpiece, the golf course.

But in contradiction of the estate's other leisure-oriented amenities, Lasker was apparently more interested in tormenting his golfing guests than entertaining them. For in addition to being Chicago's most exclusive course, Mill Road Farm was also the area's toughest, featuring a USGA difficulty rating of 76.32 and playing to an estimated 7,000 yards—an almost unheard-of length at the time of its 1926 opening. Including over 110 bunkers, this U.S. Open-style monster was challenged by many of the era's top players including 1928 U.S. Open champion Johnny Farrell (who named it among his top 10 favorite courses) and the legendary Bobby Jones, who reportedly called it one of the three best layouts in the country.

How tough did Mill Road Farm play? From the time of its inception, Lasker offered a $500 prize to anyone capable of breaking par from the back tees—and didn't pay off until 1934 when Tommy Armour scraped it around in 69. That same year, Grantland Rice, in his series for *The American Golfer* on the nation's greatest holes, stated flatly that "The private course of Mr. Al Lasker has more than its share of thrillers when it comes to meeting par on equal terms."

As a result of Mill Road Farm's extreme privacy, Rice's reference was one of the very few ever to appear in print, making it virtually impossible for the modern researcher to accurately pin down the layout's precise yardages. What few mentions did appear presented an overall length of either 7,000 or 7,100 yards, with par generally listed at 70 or, occasionally, 72. Unfortunately, as the course had only three one-shotters and two holes measuring well over 550 yards, a par of 70 would not have been possible, at least in its original configuration.

For the record then, the yardages presented here are carefully-calculated estimates, scaled down piece-by-piece (using a round total of 7,000 yards) from the lone aerial photograph of the entire property known to exist. The sequence in which the holes are numbered likewise represents an educated guess, with the proximity of the Lasker mansion and several additional factors suggesting this as the most likely order of play.

Such a sequence began with a stiff 435-yard dogleg-left par-4 whose driving area was pinched by both trees and a collection of three fairway bunkers. The second, a 200-yard one-shotter, doubled back toward the mansion and offered little margin for error, placing a smile squarely upon the face of anyone fortunate enough to have come this far in only seven strokes.

In truth, the next several holes, while undoubtedly demanding, were not altogether brutal and it was here where any real scoring ground would have to be gained. The third and fourth, flanked by right-side out-of-bounds, required some precision but were neither unreasonably long nor narrow. The fifth was a bit claustrophobic but at only 340 yards, allowed one the layup option off the tee. And finally the sixth, at 485 yards, was Mill Road Farm's only real birdie hole, though a narrow fairway and large crossbunkers 75 yards shy of the green likely meant at least a full wedge third for those unable to reach the putting surface in two.

Holes seven, eight, and nine were by far the course's shortest stretch, but in no way its easiest. The seventh in particular, despite measuring only 370 yards, required a very precise approach to a green defended by both sand and overhanging trees. The eighth was more cerebral, requiring a drive over a right-side bunker if a good angle of approach were to be had. The ninth, at only 160 yards, simply offered no room for error.

If this was in fact the proper sequence of play, there was a curious yardage imbalance between the front and back nines, a discrepancy immediately highlighted by the interminable 580-yard 10th, a distinctly three-shot par-5.

The 11th and 12th, stretching 435 and 420 yards, respectively, would have fit any U.S. Open track in America. Both were narrow and tightly bunkered, requiring two long and precise shots to reach their greens in regulation. One has little trouble imagining that pars might even have represented "skins" here—particularly on a course receiving only a handful of rounds each day.

Following the equally demanding 210-yard 13th came a pair of sub-400-yard two-shotters traversing out and back from the layout's western boundary. At 390 yards, the 14th may have represented the back nine's only breather but the 15th, with 10 bunkers dotting its 375 yards, left little room for straying.

Mr. Lasker's finishers were a bit of a varied lot, beginning with the 570-yard 16th. The 385-yard 17th then featured the course's lone water hazard, a small lake located short-right of the putting surface. A tee shot positioned left could take this water largely out of play but, with one large tree standing guard, the margin for error was slight.

The 465-yard closer was an immensely difficult par-4 requiring another clear plan of action. Its challenge essentially lay in a large right-side bunker which trimmed the fairway virtually by half and required nearly 240 yards of air time to be carried. Assuming this hazard was avoided, one faced a 200-plus-yard approach to the most severely bunkered green on the course. If not, number 18 simply became a par-5—or worse.

Mill Road Farm was altered somewhat in its later years with some reports claiming that it was shortened to less than 6,600 yards. If such stories were accurate, this modified version likely wasn't seen by too many, for aside from its general exclusivity, the course's days were fast becoming numbered. As the Depression lingered and the era of opulent living fell further into the past, Albert Lasker toned down his lifestyle and eventually donated the estate to the University of Chicago. After World War II, the land was sold off and subdivided and by 1950, had begun the transition to the residential neighborhood that exists today.

How Mill Road Would Measure Up Today

Still a monster.

Consider that those limited reports from which this profile was gleaned make no mention of such tough-course staples as hard, slick greens or formidable rough, suggesting that with the right conditioning, it potentially could play even tougher today. Would it be ranked in people's Top 100? Sure—if anyone with a vote ever got an invitation to see it.

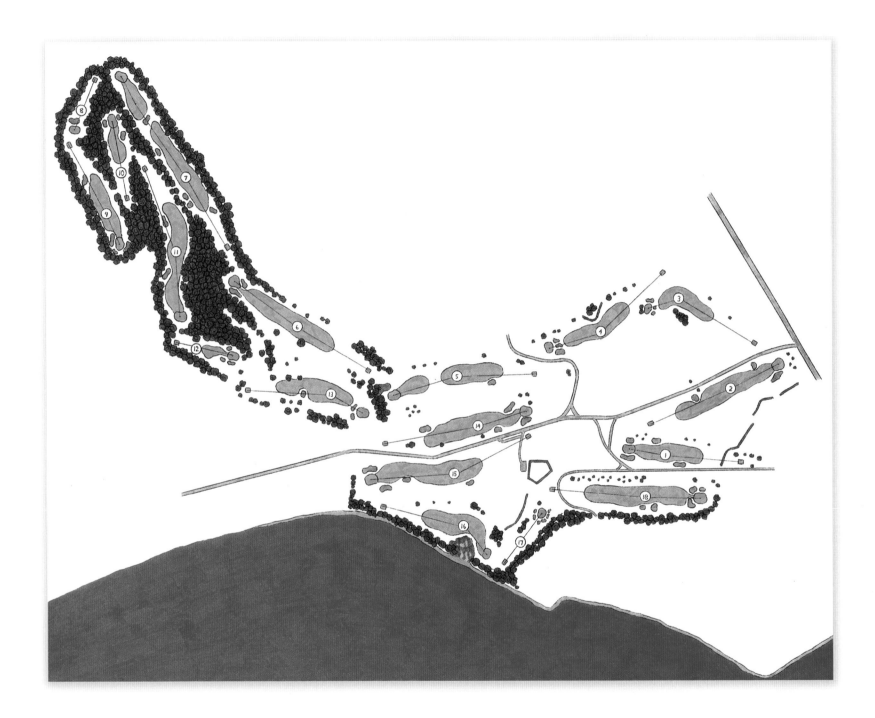

YORKTOWN (River View)

319	398	302	390	403	435	510	143	308	3208	210	418	165	341	410	470	316	187	431	2948	6156
4	4	4	4	4	4	5	3	4	36	3	4	3	4	4	5	4	3	4	34	70

YORKTOWN COUNTRY CLUB

YORKTOWN, VA

River View Course 1926 / 6156 yards Par-70

Given the logistics of the undertaking, it is hardly uncommon for golf courses to be built upon tracts of land bearing some degree of historical importance. The Sea Island Club in Georgia, for example, for years noted an ancient slave graveyard not far from its clubhouse, and the seventh at San Francisco Golf Club sits adjacent to the site of the last formal duel fought upon American soil. But without question, no American course—perhaps no layout anywhere—can even begin to match the Yorktown Country Club for historical importance, or, for that matter, in the grandiosity of its plans and the untimeliness of its unfortunate demise.

Yorktown, as anyone recalling his high school history knows, became indelibly inked in the annals of modern history when on October 19, 1781, British troops under General Cornwallis marched through a gauntlet of American and French forces, their surrender officially ending the war for American Independence. The rather attractive acreage upon which this surrender took place was a high plateau some 70 feet above the adjacent York River. Years later it would see further military action, its battlements being partially destroyed by British troops during the War of 1812, then rebuilt and utilized by both Confederate and Union forces during the Civil War.

The idea of developing a majestic recreational facility on this hallowed ground apparently enjoyed backing fairly early in the twentieth century. But it wasn't until the 1920s, when much of the immediately adjacent battlefield was purchased through private subscription, that some ambitious plans were finally laid. Envisioned was a revolutionary concept, a recreational and political center designed to bring together the world's great dignitaries in a spirit of cooperation and relaxation—sort of an early-day United Nations with country club facilities thrown in.

In its original conception, the development was to be made up of three separate components:

The World Forum, a planned 15,000-person auditorium-like facility built to serve as a meeting place for diplomats and dignitaries, to be surrounded by a village of libraries, historical buildings, and residential accommodations.

The Yorktown Manor Hotel, a world-class resort hostelry designed to take advantage of the area's moderate year-round climate and central North-South location.

The Yorktown Country Club, a top-flight recreational facility featuring golf, tennis, and all manner of equestrian and water sports, its membership by invitation only, to be made up of high-ranking American and foreign government officials, dignitaries, and those of social or historical prominence.

The Yorktown Manor Hotel was itself quite a story, initially conceived as a 300-room colonial-style extravaganza to be designed by the famous architectural firm of McKim, Mead & White. By the time the cornerstone was laid in April of 1926, however, those plans had been replaced by a more modest version which, in the end, would itself never reach completion. The World Forum too would never materialize, with little evidence to suggest that it ever progressed beyond the rough planning stages. But the Country Club was an entirely different story.

To create a superior golf facility, the club's organizers approached William Flynn, who promptly surveyed the roughly 2,000 acres at his disposal and declared them, as seems obligatory of the time, "ideal." The original plan was for Flynn to design 36 holes and while only the slightly-shorter River View Course was actually constructed, the 6,177-yard Lake View was fully drawn.

There is little doubt that the River View, though offering several outstanding holes, does not belong upon the very top shelf of Flynn's work. Yet it was an enjoyable and most interesting design, routed through tall Virginia pines and stands of ambiance-enhancing Scotch broom, a crop apparently imported during the colonial era to feed the British army horses. It was also a layout which held the distinction not only of utilizing the historic battlefield terrain but actually requiring several shots to be played over or around the remains of its fortifications. A booklet published by the club in the late 1920s described the course's landscape this way:

"The bristling ramparts and deep moats and sinuous trenches, constructed by the opposing armies during weeks of siege, are today practically as they were in 1781, except that they were used and strengthened by both the Confederate and Union troops during the campaign of 1862.

"At yonder point, General Washington had his headquarters. Over this moat, the gallant Marquis de Lafayette lead (*sic*) his troops to attack. These ramparts were captured by Count de Rochambeau's veterans..."

Presidents
Pershing
awarded
honorary
ual club
known.
ip.

, its tee
, leav-

				Hole names	
4		10	30	Magruder	3
4		11	413	McClellan	4
4		12	105	Town of York	3
4		13	341	Pocahontas	4
4		14	420	Nelson	4
4		15	400	Count de Grasse	4
5		16	30	Hamilton's Attack	4
3		17	187	The Redoubts	3
4		18	431	The American Fleet	4
36		in			33

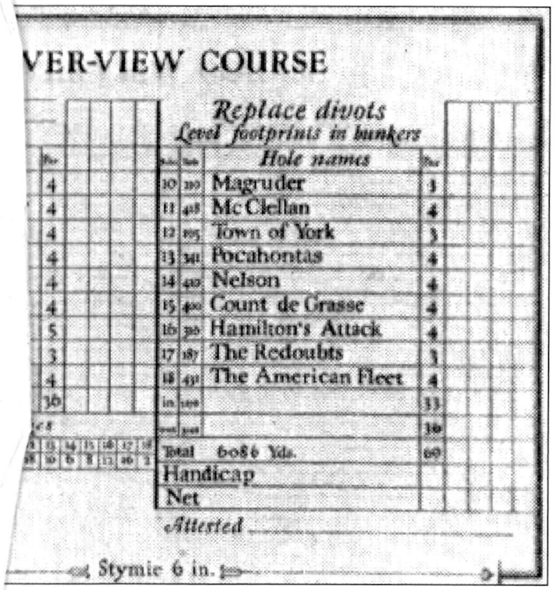

VER-VIEW COURSE

Replace divots
Level footprints in bunkers

Total 6086 Yds.
Handicap
Net
Attested _____
Stymie 6 in.

River View Course scorecard,
highlighting the course's patriotic
theme. (U.S. National Parks Service)

Follo...ing several more holes of moderate length, the River View closed with three exciting finishers that would have held their own almost anywhere. The 16th, in fact, was quite spectacular, a 316-yard par-4 stretched out along the bluffs above the York River. Here was a classic decision-making scenario as the player faced three distinct options: lay up safely in a wide section of short fairway (leaving a full-shot second), drive toward a narrower section pinched by a deep indentation of the bluff (leaving a short, relatively easy pitch), or boldly attempt to drive the green, carrying the ravine-like indentation in the process.

The 17th was another nature-menaced hole, running inland some 187 yards to a green perched dangerously close to a rough stretch of jungle. The finisher, the River View's second longest par-4 at 431 yards, closed things out with an historic touch, its tee placed back among the ramparts, its well-bunkered green located within walking distance of the hotel.

Routed among the remains of our nation's most famous Revolutionary War battle, steeped in patriotic ambiance that included holes adorned entirely with Revolutionary War names, the Yorktown Country Club was surely one of the most remarkable golf projects ever undertaken. Sadly, Depression-era financial problems and the failure of the World Forum concept to garner international support led to an early demise for the entire enterprise. Unlike so many doomed courses, though, Yorktown did not become a strip mall or housing development, instead being incorporated into today's Colonial National Historic Park. Its departure did, however, engender one significant mystery: the whereabouts of the Duke of York's silver cup, an heirloom of unique value and symbolism which vanished, like the club itself, long before its time.

How Yorktown Would Measure Up Today

Depending upon one's perspective, as either an incredible piece of history or a sacrilegious corruption of some of America's most famous land. As a golf course, it likely would be seen as little more than an old, character-filled resort layout, though the three finishing holes (and number 16 in particular) would still draw their fair share of attention.

ALSO BY WILLIAM FLYNN

Among William Flynn's other reportedly lost courses, there is little in the way of concrete documentation. His first-ever design, for example, a 1911 nine-holer in Heartwellville, Vermont, was apparently the private estate course referred to in occasional period articles as the Kilkare Golf Club. It, most certainly, is long gone.

Though the golf media paid an enormous amount of attention to the booming state of Florida throughout the 1920s, Flynn's work there is sometimes even more difficult to trace. Notable were two frequently-listed facilities which may never have existed at all, the Floridale Golf Club and the Miami Beach Polo Club. To the former, no reference was made in any period publication or guidebook, not even of its location, an unmapped town called Milford. For the latter, a check of local planning departments and historical societies revealed the well-documented presence of the Polo Club but no record of it ever possessing a regulation golf course.

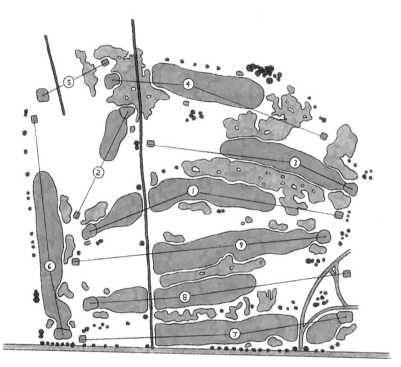

The lost Blue nine at Atlantic City CC.

One well-documented loss from the architect's portfolio was the third or Blue nine at the Atlantic City (NJ) Country Club. A par-34, 3,075-yard layout in 1933, it was every bit as good as the adjoining (and still-extant) 18, winding through acres of open, sandy terrain and featuring par-4s of 409, 426, 428, and 435 yards among its more demanding holes. Somewhat similar in style to Flynn's Boca Raton work, its land today houses both the club's practice facility and a residential neighborhood.

Thankfully, the vast majority of William Flynn's verifiable layouts remain in play at the time of this writing. But the most significant ones that don't—Yorktown, Boca Raton, and Mill Road Farm—represent losses of a grand scale.

ATLANTIC CITY									
435	183	344	368	126	356	428	426	409	3075
4	3	4	4	3	4	4	4	4	34

WILLIAM LANGFORD

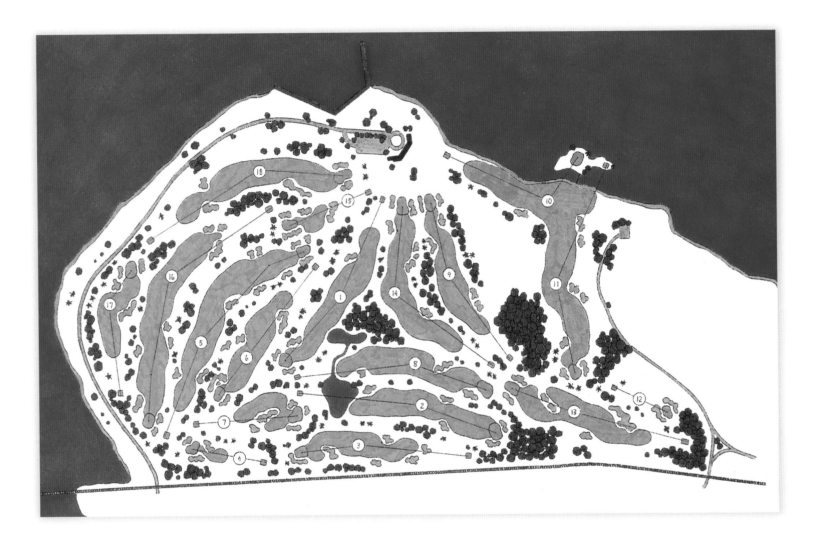

KEY WEST																				
400	435	355	150	500	325	210	415	370	3160	340	460	120	385	425	180	540	250	445	3145	6305
4	4	4	3	5	4	3	4	4	35	4	5	3	4	4	3	5	4	4	36	71

KEY WEST GOLF CLUB
KEY WEST, FL

Opened in 1925 / 6,305 yards Par-71

Key West, Florida. The southernmost point of America. A subtropical outpost finally reached by Henry Flagler's railroad in 1912. Once inhabited by Ernest Hemingway, Tennessee Williams, and Robert Frost, and latter-day pirates whose livings were made by salvaging sunken ships of which they themselves had frequently done the sinking. Home to countless images of frontiers, romance, and intrigue.

And home, quite remarkably, to one very interesting golf course.

Of course, once upon a time Key West hardly even seemed a part of the United States, its stark geographic isolation placing it little closer to the mainstream of American life than Cuba, the Bahamas, or several other in-lying Caribbean entities. But along came Mr. Flagler's $50 million folly, a truly amazing feat of over-water engineering, and thus linked to civilization, the little island prospered.

With Florida's 1920s emergence as America's favorite winter playground came Key West's corresponding development as a place known for its topflight fishing, remarkable sunsets, and casual, laid-back lifestyle. Its proximity to Cuba—only 90 miles by ferry—certainly didn't hurt, as America's uninhibited southern neighbor soon established itself as the Caribbean's den of iniquity, its beaches, nightlife, and gambling regularly drawing thousands of visitors through the Keys in transit.

It was in the middle of the '20s, just as the Florida boom was taking off, that locals, hoping to keep some of that traveling affluence in town for a while, conceived the idea of a golf course. The challenges, though, were many, not the least of which being the island's coral rock foundation, a base pronounced ideal for bridge building but rather ill-suited to growing fairways and greens.

But the Roaring Twenties was a time of unbridled optimism, a period when all manner of technological breakthroughs made golf course construction possible in all sorts of inhospitable locales. At Key West the answer came in the form of dynamite, the explosive being used to blast the coral from the fairways, the powdered remains then being used for subsoil. And as expensive and time-consuming as this process may have been, the entrepreneurial idea of golf in Key West soon became a reality.

Financed by a municipal bond issue, the locals solved their second problem—where to find enough usable acreage in so small a locale—by purchasing the adjacent Stock Island, a landmass smaller than Key West itself but large enough to house a well-planned golf course. And to design such a layout, they then hired a popular Chicago-based architect named William Langford.

A representative view of the flat, sun-drenched Key West landscape. (*Golf Illustrated*)

Langford, a Yale graduate, was a highly prolific designer, once claiming to have worked on over 250 courses in his career. Together with his partner and construction foreman Theodore Moreau, he built extensively throughout the Midwest and Florida during the '20s and '30s, his work often featuring elevated and steeply bunkered green complexes. Lacking the natural contour to follow this approach at Key West, he instead turned out a cerebral layout which utilized 10 doglegs and heavy bunkering to create numerous strategic challenges. And, as something of a calling card, it managed to feature one of America's all-time most unique holes as well.

Langford's Key West creation began with a pair of long par-4s, both of which provided a fair degree of driving latitude within the brush-covered, jungle-like landscape. The third and fourth then proceeded westward, parallel to the East Coast Railway tracks before the par-5 fifth swung back to the northeast, its rightward sweep and diagonal bunkers tempting the player to get overly courageous with his second.

Another noteworthy front-nine hole was the 210-yard, par-3 seventh. Easily the course's longest one-shotter, it provided the rare accommodation of two distinct layup areas for those unable to reach the distant putting surface. For the more aggressive, a tee shot carrying two large crossbunkers left an open, straight-on chip. For the conservative, a left-side layup was safer, but also brought the left greenside bunker very much into play on one's second.

Key West's classic hole was the daring and spectacular 340-yard 10th, a genuine showpiece. Doglegging nearly 90 degrees to the left, it proceeded first along Stock Island's northern

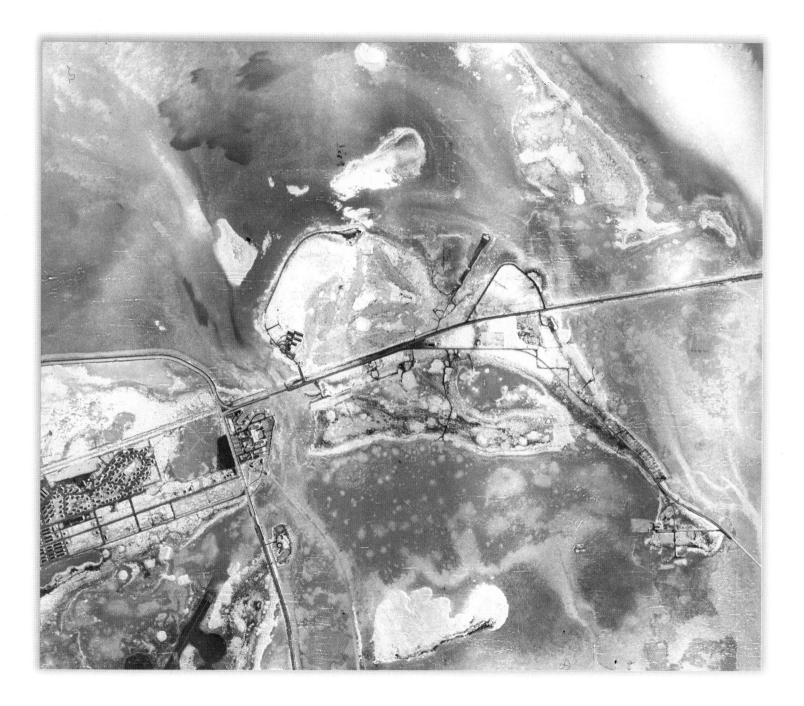

World War II-era aerial survey of Stock Island. Remains of several pre-hurricane Langford holes, club entrance road, and parking area still visible. (National Archives)

shoreline, then onto an island situated some 25 yards out in the Gulf of Mexico. For mortals, the generous width of the fairway meant that number 10's primary challenge lay in its across-the-water short-iron approach. With the island being of fairly good size and bunker-free, however, one wonders just how many big hitters found the 240-yard carry required to drive it too enticing to pass up.

Following the short par-5 11th and dangerous pitch-shot 12th came a tough and interesting finishing stretch. The 425-yard dogleg-right 14th personified this challenge, as did the layout's longest hole, the 540-yard 16th. Perhaps not so coincidentally, this man-sized three-shotter worked its way to the island's western flank, presenting those finishing late in the day with a direct view of Key West's world-famous sunset.

The par-4 closers were something of a Mutt and Jeff pair. The 250-yard 17th, only barely reaching the USGA's two-shot minimum yardage, was a thought-provoking sort, daring the player to carry a right-side bunker and head directly for the green or lay up left, where two more bunkers obscured one's second shot. The 445-yard 18th, on the other hand, frequently required two woods and generally yielded pars sparingly.

In addition to being a revenue-producing commodity, the Stock Island property also served as the area's prime recreation facility with a park and baseball field situated upon its eastern boundary. The club also featured a full practice area (located between holes nine and ten), a fine clubhouse, and a large boat basin located immediately to its north.

What evidence exists of the course's untimely demise suggests that it took place in stages. In all likelihood it was the enormous 1926 hurricane that devastated Florida's East Coast and ended the great land boom that began the slide, a suggestion supported by the 1927 American Annual Golf Guide which listed the club as having been diminished to nine holes. The Depression came next, followed by a 1935 Gulf Coast hurricane—Key West's worst ever—which likely polished off for good whatever remained of Langford's visionary layout. Today an 18-hole Rees Jones facility exists on the Stock Island site, a fine public course but not in any way related to the island's fascinating and short-lived original.

How Key West Would Measure Up Today

Surprisingly well, all things considered.

Whether by design or happenstance, Langford left a good deal of room behind nearly all of his tees, allowing for the modern lengthening needed on terrain too flat to utilize contouring as a means of maintaining its challenge. The 10th hole in particular might have benefitted from this expansion as moving its tee back and to the left likely would have created an even more spectacular test. That is, assuming that the green was built on genuine terra firma and not a mangrove clump destined to disintegrate over time, hurricanes notwithstanding.

CHARLES BLAIR MACDONALD & SETH RAYNOR

DEEPDALE																				
460	400	340	420	160	480	420	130	400	3210	390	420	220	350	440	190	540	340	420	3310	6520
5	4	4	4	3	5	4	3	4	36	4	4	3	4	4	3	5	4	4	35	71

DEEPDALE GOLF CLUB

GREAT NECK, NY

Opened in 1926 / 6,520 yards Par-71

For those well acquainted with the history of golf in America (or simply reading this volume in sequential order) the name of Charles Blair Macdonald is hardly a new one. A tall, barrel-chested man, Macdonald cast an enormous shadow over the game, both literally and figuratively, from the moment he returned from collegiate study in Scotland until his quiet death in Southampton, New York, at the ripe old age of 83.

Though a lifetime resident of the United States, Macdonald was not actually American, having been born to a Scottish father and Canadian mother just across the border in Niagara Falls, Ontario (this little-remembered fact allowing A.W. Tillinghast to bill himself for years as "The Dean of American-born architects"). Macdonald did, however, grow up in Chicago before pursuing his higher education at St. Andrew's University where, surrounded by men like Old Tom Morris and David Strath, he became both a proficient golfer and a lifelong lover of the royal and ancient game. Upon returning to Illinois in 1875, he then endured what he later referred to as "The Dark Ages," a 17-year period in which the complete lack of golf facilities in the Chicago area allowed him little more opportunity to play than beating makeshift balls around an abandoned army training ground.

Though Macdonald's general contributions to the game's growth and prosperity were many (among them leading the effort to found the United States Golf Association in 1894), the focus of this book is on golf courses and architecture and here more than anywhere, C.B. shone.

His initial foray into course design came in 1892 when, through little more than his compelling personality and considerable force of will, he wrangled up enough interest among his Second City stockbroker friends to found the Chicago Golf Club, building it a nine-hole course in suburban Belmont. Later, after moving to New York in 1900, he became enamored with the idea of creating America's first truly great course, a facility which would replicate and perhaps even improve upon the classic holes of the British Isles. The result, after years of organizing, site searching, and planning was The National Golf Links of America, surely the most influential golf course ever constructed by man.

His reputation as a master architect thus secure for posterity, Macdonald was never again especially active in the discipline. After 1911, in fact, he never built more than two courses in a year and even then, tended to rely more upon the abilities of his construction foreman and hand-picked protégé, Seth Raynor, than his own efforts in the field. Indeed, of the 15 or so projects upon which Macdonald's name would subsequently be attached, it can be comfortably suggested that Raynor was actually the primary designer of at least half, and given what records have been unearthed, even that estimate may be somewhat conservative.

After 1920, Macdonald's role appears to have declined even further, dissolving into something resembling the ceremonial. While there is no doubt of his direct involvement in the building of Bermuda's Mid Ocean Club in 1924, Raynor clearly appears to have completed virtual solo work at The Greenbrier's Number Three Course, Long Island's Creek Club, and Yale University, where a 1925 issue of the *Yale Alumni Weekly* stated as much in pleasant but unambiguous terms. This understood, it then seems apparent that Macdonald's final active design effort—one in which his involvement genuinely seems to have been significant— was at Great Neck, New York, in 1926, at an ultra-private club known as Deepdale.

Deepdale was the brainchild of Mr. William K. Vanderbilt II, scion of the great Vanderbilt railroad fortune and an avid Long Island sportsman. At the urging of several friends, he elected to convert a 200-acre section of his summer estate on Lake Success into a golf course reserved strictly for their usage, a course which, given the obvious trappings of the Vanderbilt wealth, could only answer to the description "second to none."

While records do not exist to specifically document Macdonald's involvement, two items suggest that he did actively join Raynor (and his protégé Charles Banks) in developing the Lake Success site. First, as a matter of propriety, it seems unlikely that a man of his stature would take a commission from the likes of William Vanderbilt, then provide something less than his best effort by farming the project out to his associates. Perhaps more importantly, the Deepdale design just *felt* more like Macdonald, its bunkering more wildly shaped than Raynor's quasi-geometric approach, its green complexes showing little of the squarish designs that Raynor so frequently employed. But whoever was ultimately responsible for the finished product, Deepdale was, by the universal acclaim of the few who saw it, sensational.

Playing fairly long (in 1920s terms) at 6,520 yards with a par of 71, the course began modestly with a short, straightaway par-5. Things toughened immediately at the second though, where the tee ball had to carry a large, wild bunker, hopefully favoring the right side of the

Charles Blair Macdonald: architect, champion, egotist, and pioneer supreme. (*Golf Illustrated*)

fairway. From there one faced a mid-iron approach to a triangular green angling from right-to-left and nearly surrounded by both sand and trees.

The third, little more than a drive-and-pitch at 340 yards, was known as Horseshoe and while its curving putting surface could not truly be considered of the boomerang style, the incursion of a small bunker rear-center certainly demanded accuracy in the placement of the approach.

The 160-yard fifth was the first of a particularly fine set of one-shotters. Known by the club's name, Deepdale, it was played to a small, narrow green which was all but surrounded by several rather artistic bunkers—hazards not dissimilar in style to many built by architects such as Pete Dye half a century later.

Interior of the very-private Deepdale club-house, famous for the on-scale wall mural depicting C.B. Macdonald's original course layout. (*Golf Illustrated*)

The outward half's second par-3, the 130-yard eighth, bore a first-glance resemblance to Macdonald's original Short hole but apparently lacked the horseshoe-shaped ridge sculpted into its putting surface. At 400 yards, the par-4 ninth then required a particularly well-played drive to carry a large, low-lying area and avoid six fairway bunkers of differing size and angles. That accomplished, what remained was relatively simple: a slightly uphill approach to a large green offering several difficult pin placements.

Deepdale's inward half began with the 390-yard Punchbowl 10th, a somewhat-forgiving design wherein a green housed in a natural depression generally welcomed slightly off-line approaches kicking down from the surrounding hillsides.

The 420-yard 11th, a replica modeled after the famous Alps hole at Prestwick, was far less welcoming. The Alps concept—that of a blind long-iron second played over large mounding, generally to an elevated putting surface—was a tremendously demanding one, as embodied both by the infamous Scottish original and Macdonald's particularly nasty replicas at both The National and The Lido. The version built at Deepdale was apparently no less difficult and, as such, was rated among the layout's most memorable holes.

The 420-yard 18th, routed along the shore of the aptly-named Lake Success. (*The American Golfer*)

Following a typically strong Biarritz at the 12th and a slight respite at 13, the 440-yard 14th was Deepdale's only hole to include anything resembling another Macdonald/ Raynor favorite, the Road-style green. Was this actually a Road replica despite being named Garden? The hole's straightaway path suggests not, but the green complex—guarded front-left by a small bunker and back right by a long, narrow one—does beg the question.

One place where genesis was not up for debate was at the 190-yard Redan 15th, a splendid par-3 which drew frequent and favorable comparison to The National's fourth, generally considered the finest Redan replica of them all.

Following the distinctly three-shot 16th came one of Deepdale's more interesting holes, the 340-yard 17th. Laid out along the westernmost spur of Lake Success, it was, to a large degree, a left-to-right version of Macdonald's Cape hole wherein the player's selection of a target line depended upon finding just the right balance of confidence and ego. On this particular version, a ball played safely left meant a bunker-inhibited second while anything missed to the right was drowned.

The 420-yard uphill 18th was even more demanding. Save for a small inlet just before the tee, the drive was not a forced carry but did need to avoid a section of lake which cut into play near the 270-yard mark. Short of this point the fairway was quite wide but featured sand left and the prospect of a tree-obscured second from the right, making straightness imperative.

Naturally, so wonderful a course drew the interest of a great many players and as a result, Vanderbilt was not long in yielding to peer pressure, turning his private plaything into a small, highly exclusive club. Its membership soon became a Who's Who of New York financial society, most of whom were also members of The National or Shinnecock Hills and used Deepdale as their "in-town" course, saving the two-hour trek out to the Hamptons for weekends and holidays. Over its nearly 30-year existence, Deepdale's roster also included an astounding eight presidents of the USGA, though its well-guarded privacy precluded taking advantage of this representation in securing any prestigious national tournaments.

But eventually, even so powerful a membership as this could mount little in the way of resistance when, in 1954, New York State chose to route the Long Island Expressway through a northern section of the course. Though a plan was considered to reconfigure the land that remained, the membership ultimately judged this unsatisfactory and sold the property, hiring Dick Wilson to build them a distinctly modern Deepdale in nearby Manhasset. Oddly, Vanderbilt's original land was then purchased by the Lake Success Country Club, who continue to play golf there, though on a completely redesigned layout. With a famous mural depicting Macdonald's original design no longer on display in the Lake Success clubhouse, all that remains of the halcyon days are the vintage Vanderbilt-era lockers, a faint reminder of a time and a golf course not easily replaced.

How Deepdale Would Measure Up Today

Though hardly a National, Winged Foot, or Shinnecock Hills, Deepdale would still rank as one of the New York area's best, particularly since staunch avoidance of the public eye always seems to boost a club's reputation disproportionately. Still, with inevitable lengthening to perhaps 6,800 yards and the sixth hole reclassified to a long par-4, this character-oozing design would be quite the par-70 test—and with age, image, and tradition on its side, a likely gate-crasher into most Top 100s.

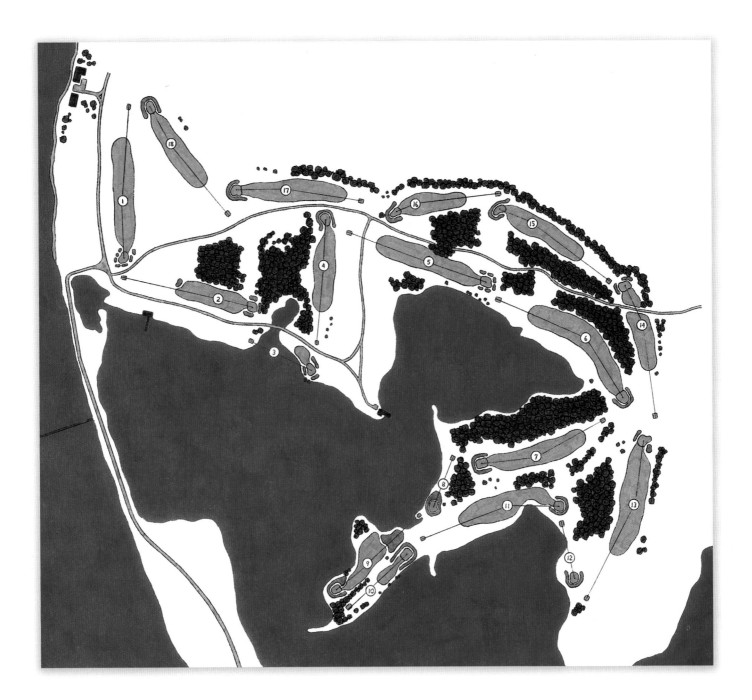

GIBSON ISLAND																				
409	380	181	348	425	414	398	157	330	3042	220	362	161	420	381	359	255	406	354	2918	5960
4	4	3	4	4	4	4	3	4	34	3	4	3	5	4	4	4	4	4	35	69

GIBSON ISLAND COUNTRY CLUB
GIBSON ISLAND, MD

Opened in 1923 / 5,960 yards Par-69

The fantasies of an avid golfer are both fun to ponder and wholly predictable: a hole-in-one, a round at St. Andrew's with Jack Nicklaus, two putts from 20 feet to win the U.S. Open—and these, relatively speaking, are the plausible ones. For deep inside every player lies some version of the same basic dream: buy an island, build the ideal course, and then invite all of one's friends to come visit, to play, to build houses and stay a while. Unfortunately, modern real estate prices being what they are, even today's well-off are generally relegated to living vicariously through the handful of affluent men who, many years ago, actually possessed both the imagination and the wherewithal to put such grandiose plans into action.

Mr. W. Stuart Symington of Baltimore, Maryland was just such a person. Believing that his home state was lacking a golf course of genuinely championship caliber, he took the rather bold step of purchasing Gibson Island, a 950-acre expanse located 19 miles south of town, where the Magothy River empties into Chesapeake Bay. He then hired C.B. Macdonald and Seth Raynor (as well as the legendary Olmsted Brothers landscaping firm) to create for him a golfer's paradise: a private, geographically-isolated retreat that would feature 36 first-class holes, a tennis and beach club, boat dockage, and 423 real estate lots ranging in size from .4 to 4.4 acres. By 1922 the plans were complete and construction began, with an initial nine holes opening in 1923, then a second nine in 1924.

Though there is much to suggest that Gibson Island's on-course design work was done primarily by Raynor, more than the usual scant evidence exists to document some substantial Macdonald involvement as well. Early club records, for example, indicate that C.B. did visit the site and quote him regarding "the golf course which I roughly sketched." Olmsted company records, however, several times referred to the course "as laid out by Raynor," suggesting perhaps that Macdonald routed the layout, then allowed his trusted associate to take over from there.

Whatever the case, Gibson Island's first course offered, by any measure, some of the most spectacular golf holes ever built. Yet with a total length of only 5,960 yards, it fell well shy of genuine, full-scale greatness. Was this Macdonald and Raynor's original intention? Doubtful, for a 1922 Olmsted company general map of the island clearly indicated plans for a longer and more difficult track, a par-70 affair following the very same routing but measuring a stout 6,327 yards. Furthermore, a 1924 *The American Golfer* article noted the 5,970-yard layout but stated that the course would be lengthened "as soon as the turf of the fairways becomes mature." In the end, this planned expansion never did take place, leaving a par-69 course which, though exceptionally memorable, could not truly be placed at the forefront of the Macdonald/Raynor portfolio.

1920s aerial of the island's entrance.
Second and Redan third hole at center,
17th green slightly to the left.
(Gibson Island CC)

The layout began in full-sized fashion with a 409-yard par-4, then turned westward at the 380-yard second, a mid-length two-shotter played to one of many greens surrounded at least 75% by sand. It is worth noting at this point that Gibson Island was frequently cited for the great depth of its bunkers, with some greenside hazards running as deep as 15 feet!

The third was the club's first replica hole and a dandy: a 181-yard reverse Redan (i.e., green sloping front-left to back-right) angled across an inlet of the Magothy Narrows. Though other Redans have involved carries over water, it is doubtful that any has been built with the water so much in play, in this case both short and right of the putting surface.

Following the 348-yard fourth, the course returned to the coastline with the 425-yard fifth, a long par-4 played to another particularly well-bunkered green, with the waters of Red House Cove lurking close by.

One prominent difference indicated upon the Olmsted map from the layout "as built" came at the 398-yard par-4 seventh. Here a cluster of dead-center fairway bunkers modeled after the famous Principal's Nose at St. Andrew's apparently died on the drawing board, leaving a firm but not terribly fancy two-shotter routed through thick stands of trees.

And then the fun started.

Having wended its way onto a narrow peninsula some 700 yards long, Gibson Island's next three holes represented a Hall-of-Fame run, the likes of which have seldom been seen concurrently or since. The 157-yard Short eighth began the proceedings, playing to a dough-nut-type green placed perilously close to the waterline.

The 330-yard ninth was not only spectacular but classically strategic, its drive offering the player a short, fairly-wide layup area or daring him to hit a full driver into a narrow section of fairway pinched between trees and the water. Given the hole's relative shortness, the layup may well have been the smarter play, though an aggressive ball well-placed did result in a less-impeded pitch for one's second.

The 220-yard 10th worked back in from the point and was likely rivaled only by the fifth at Fishers Island as the most spectacularly situated rendition of the Biarritz ever done. With the waters of the Narrows lapping at its right edge, this was a standard Biarritz design save for one notable difference: instead of the usual squarish, geometrically-precise bunkers, it sported one continuous hazard which continued around behind the putting surface in a giant, unforgiving horseshoe. Strangely, this rather novel bunkering style was used an unheard-of 11 times at Gibson Island, likely suggesting some straying from the original Macdonald/ Raynor plans during construction.

The course turned inland following the 362-yard 11th and short 12th, and it must be admitted that for the most part, Gibson Island's best holes were now in the rear view. Still, the 420-yard 13th would have made a demanding par-4 (were it not played as a par-5 on this length-starved early layout), and the tiny 255-yard 16th must have been a conversation piece. Though eminently driveable for longer hitters, its tiny green was heavily menaced by a very deep bunker angled to tempt the drawn, running approach.

After the long par-4 17th came the closer, a 354-yard two-shotter of curious background. In reality, the hole was a rather dull, straightaway affair played to a green whose bunkering vaguely favored a left-side tee shot. The Olmsted map, however, clearly illustrated a fascinating 404-yard Alps replica wherein a drive played across the far reaches of an angled crossbunker opened an approach shot free of the blindness imposed by a large front-left mound. Why Raynor and/or his construction crew passed on this surefire classic in favor of a shorter, far less inspiring finisher is an enduring mystery.

Though the Depression would ultimately end Stuart Symington's 36-hole dream altogether, it is a curious footnote that the club closed the outlying nine holes of the first course in 1928, well prior to the October 1929 stock market crash. The stated reason was a problem with wind blowing sand from bunkers on the exposed seaside sections. The result was the slightly reconfigured layout which remains today, a nine-holer incorporating several inland originals, none of them spectacular.

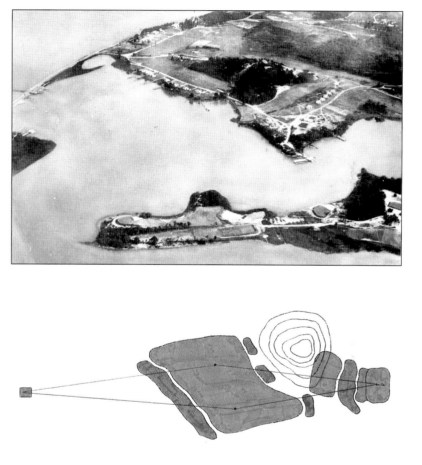

Aerial view of the front nine, featuring the Redan third (upper middle) and the peninsula eighth, ninth, and tenth, surely among the most spectacular golf holes ever built.
(Gibson Island CC)

Original plan for number 18, requiring a gutsy right-side tee shot to avoid a mound-obscured approach.

As a noteworthy aside, Raynor's plans for the never-built Number Two course showed a fine 6,192-yard par-70 track which offered, among other things, a double-fairway par-4 (the 405-yard fourth), a gorgeous 130-yard Short 16th (its doughnut green backed flush to the waters of Chesapeake Bay) and the 386-yard 17th, a bunkerless dogleg-right also snuggled close to the waterline.

But in the end, Gibson Island's intended grandeur was short-lived, its story representing a sad-but-compelling chapter in a big-thinking golfer's unfulfilled fantasy.

How Gibson Island Would Measure Up Today

Even if it had been built to its original 6,300-plus yardage, the relative blandness of Gibson Island's inland sections (plus a sub-70 par) would keep this track well below elite status. The peninsula holes, however, would be world-famous, gracing calendars, posters, and magazine covers as frequently as many vastly inferior darlings of modern-day photographers. A truly great golf course? No. But Gibson Island would fill a spot on any connoisseur's short list—and wouldn't that be enough?

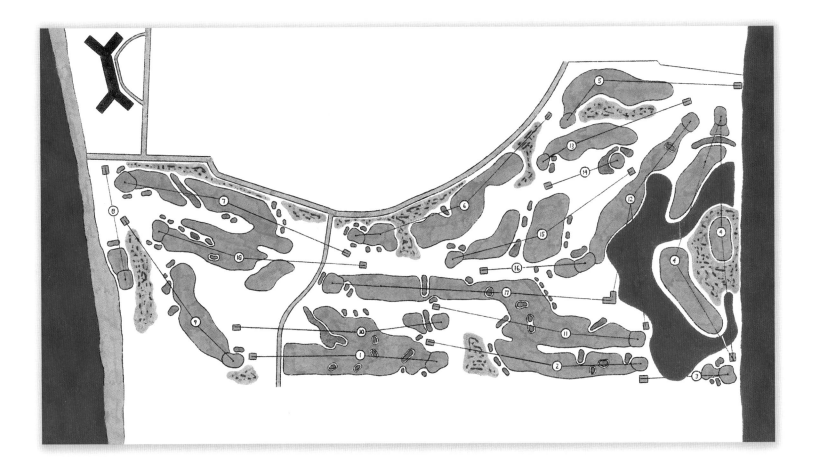

THE LIDO																			
384	421	175	466	378	493	469	234	357	3377	414	408	433	316	148	404	206	563	424	3316	6693
4	4	3	5	4	5	5	3	4	37	4	4	4	4	3	4	3	5	4	35	72

THE LIDO GOLF CLUB
LIDO BEACH, NY

Opened in 1917 / 6,693 yards Par-72

When Mr. Roger Winthrop, President of Long Island's esteemed Piping Rock Club, first approached Charles Blair Macdonald regarding the building of a golf course on 115 acres of swampland in Lido Beach, New York, Macdonald scoffed at the idea. But Winthrop was apparently quite persistent and Macdonald, his legendary ego likely intrigued by the thought of a blank canvas landfilled to his every whim, ultimately climbed aboard. What resulted—some 2,000,000 cubic yards of transported sand and nearly $800,000 dollars later—was a golf course which, had it survived, would surely stand high upon any list of the world's finest layouts.

How good was The Lido? A late 1920s survey of top professionals by New York's *Metropolitan Golfer* magazine ranked it second in America, standing behind Pine Valley but ahead of most every other famous Golden Age design. Bernard Darwin, greatest of all golf writers, called it simply "the finest course in the world." And Claude Harmon, 1948 Masters champion and, as professional at both Winged Foot and Seminole, a most learned observer, offered the ultimate praise, remarking that The Lido was in fact "the greatest golf course ever."

Whatever one's opinion, certain aspects of the club's design can be noted in a bit more objective manner. It was, for example, the first truly "man-made" golf course, its massive earth shaping rivaling that of almost any project undertaken in the modern era. It was also, without a doubt, a most authentic-looking creation, its barren, links-like expanse broken only by the six-story Lido Club, an enormous clubhouse/hotel erected at ocean's edge in 1928. And while frequently noted for its great toughness, it was also a strategic masterpiece, providing the player with numerous shotmaking options, several alternate fairways and some of the best replica holes ever built.

Like many great layouts, The Lido's first hole was a fairly simple creation, a 384-yard par-4 played downwind to a rather large and open green. The 421-yard second, which Macdonald likened to the 11th at The National, was slightly more demanding, requiring a blind drive over several crossbunkers and a somewhat more precise approach. So far, little to scream of greatness.

Wide-angle aerial showing the Lido Hotel and much of the golf course. Note the already altered seaside eighth and the Manhattan skyline faintly visible on the horizon. (*Golf Illustrated*)

The real fun began at the 175-yard third, arguably Macdonald's best adaptation of the widely-copied Eden hole at St. Andrew's. While most other versions (including Macdonald's at The National) replaced the river with one or more large bunkers, this rendition offered the waters of Reynolds Channel as a uniquely authentic replica.

Among great lost holes, few if any can match The Lido's fourth, the Channel hole, whose legend has far outlived its most challenging and heroic existence. A par-5 based largely upon the little-known 16th at Littlestone, England, it is perhaps best described by Macdonald himself, who wrote:

The beautiful Eden third, with Reynolds Channel replacing the Eden Estuary as a dangerous backdrop. (*Golf Illustrated*)

"The fourth hole is a long hole of the elbow type, which to the usual scratch player will be a three-shot hole, 510 yards in length. Both the first and second shots will be over water. The green is built high on the plateau with a deep bunker protecting it some 60 yards from the middle of the green. However, unusually long drivers, who are accurate, may play in a pocket among sand dunes by carrying 180 yards off the tee direct on the flag into a valley of fair green some 100 yards in length by 30 yards in width. Having accomplished that, they have a brassie shot for the green, making a par-4 hole of it by playing it that way."

In conclusion, he rather characteristically added:

"I think this hole will be considered the finest 510-yard hole in the world."

And he may very well have been right.

Another sensational stretch began at the 493-yard sixth, a sharp dogleg-right par-5 requiring a blind second for those long enough to attempt reaching the green in two. In a 1915 *Golf Illustrated* article detailing the course's plans, Macdonald suggested that the green complex here would be a reverse version of the ever-famous Road hole, with the hazard approximating the eponymous bunker sitting front-right instead of front-left. While such a similarity may actually have existed, the sixth instead became known as a version of "Raynor's Prized Dogleg," an original creation of Macdonald's right-hand man which was frequently replicated in Raynor's solo designs.

The 469-yard seventh, another option-oriented par-5, played directly into the sea breeze and featured a fairway-wide crossbunker to challenge one's second shot. The key to this hazard was its running on a left-to-right diagonal, thus requiring a far longer carry to reach the desired right side of the fairway and its resultant wide-open pitch.

Side view of the third green showing the famous fourth in the background. The "safe" left-side fairway appears beyond the foot-bridge, the dangerous right-side route directly on line with the distant water tower.
(Golf Illustrated)

Now, literally at water's edge, the player faced the diabolically difficult eighth. In its early years, this 234-yard par-3 arguably represented the Macdonald/Raynor team's most daunting version of the famous Biarritz hole, a strong statement considering the enormous difficulty of Raynor's Fishers Island or Yale University creations, among others. But here was a greensite so naturally well-situated as to require none of the traditional left and right bunker pairs. Instead, the standard swale-fronted green complex was flanked right by the beach (and, at high tide, the waters of the Atlantic) and left by the sort of sand-and-reed-strewn waste area which comprised much of the property's unmaintained acreage. Also, this oceanfront version's constant right-to-left breeze often required the player to aim their tee shot well out over the beach, a gutsy proposition even for the world's best.

Curiously, the eighth also "enjoyed" the rare distinction of being lost twice, once earlier on, when storm damage and/or the construction of the adjoining beach club forced its shortening to 165 yards, and again when the course closed its doors for good. The interim version, though no longer truly a Biarritz, featured a forced carry over sand to something of an island green. Not quite as difficult perhaps, but an interesting hole nonetheless.

The 357-yard ninth, which Macdonald likened to the 17th at The National, featured more simple but highly-effective strategy. From the right side of the fairway (a point requiring a nearly 200-yard carry of sand to reach), a player could literally roll his second onto the green. From the vastly safer left side, on the other hand, he would be lucky to stop even a well-struck approach upon the shallow, slightly-elevated putting surface.

The eighth hole, circa 1925: already shortened to 160 yards but still quite dangerous.
(Golf Illustrated)

The 414-yard 10th was an Alps rendition, a copy of the original Prestwick design with which Macdonald was especially enamored. Referring to a 1901 "discussion" of golf's best holes in the British magazine *Golf Illustrated*, he emphatically stated that:

"...a large majority of the first-class players considered this the best two-shot hole in the world and time has not in any measure altered that opinion."

Planning The Lido's version slightly longer to account for the new, livelier Haskell ball, Macdonald must have been pleased with the outcome as it drew praise comparable to that of his previously well-received replica at The National, if not the Prestwick original.

Like most top layouts, The Lido provided a wonderful set of finishers, beginning with the 433-yard Punch Bowl 12th, as difficult a par-4 as one might imagine in the era of hickory shafts and sane golf balls. Doglegging right around the waters of the man-made lagoon, it first required a massive tee shot carefully measured against the left-to-right ocean crosswind, then a stout second to reach a green nestled snugly among the dunes, beyond a deep cross-bunker.

View of the 11th hole also shows the 17th fairway (left) and mounds backing the 10th green (right). All manufactured, right down to the hand-planted reeds. (*Golf Illustrated*)

Following the drive-and-pitch 13th (modeled after Macdonald's own Knoll hole at Piping Rock) and Short 14th (requiring a bit of finesse straight downwind) came the splendid 15th, a strong 404-yarder played straight back into the breeze. Here the player faced another clear driving option: play to the right, into a wide area of fairway from which two greenside bunkers came very much into play, or left, across a line of three traps, for a less-impeded second.

Rear view of the green at the dangerous 433-yard 12th, lagoon visible at upper left. Also note the green complex of the Short 14th at upper right. (*Golf Illustrated*)

Macdonald, considering the Redan 15th at North Berwick to be the finest one-shot hole in the world, advocated the inclusion of its replica on every golf course and at The Lido it came in the form of the 206-yard 16th. Though not viewed in the same light as the fourth at The National, this version was certainly taxing, though its greater-than-standard length was mitigated somewhat by the favorable sea breeze.

Though Macdonald called the massive 563-yard 17th a "composite" hole, it was listed on the scorecard as "long" and mirrored the challenges of the so-named 14th at St. Andrew's quite well. Here the player had to decide whether to attempt to carry an enormous cross-bunker some 125 yards shy of the putting surface with his second, no small feat in the face of that ever-present headwind.

But even with so many great holes, and despite the presence of the legendary fourth, it is likely that no hole at The Lido was greater or of more historic value than the finisher, the 424-yard par-4 18th. The story, of course, is well-known. In 1914, at Macdonald's urging, the British magazine *Country Life* ran a contest to see who could design the ideal two-shot hole. Selected from among 81 entries was a rather wild triple-fairway creation by the then-less-famous Dr. Alister MacKenzie and it was this design, altered slightly to fit the local terrain, that Macdonald used for the finisher at The Lido. An option-laden affair, the Home hole played dead into the wind and offered several distinct driving targets, a long second across a line of angled bunkers and a large, heavily-contoured green.

So, was The Lido actually the "greatest golf course ever"? There are likely none among us so bold as to make that call, but several things are certain: it was a genuine, top-shelf masterpiece, a very tough but highly flexible golf course offering an enormous variety of holes, few less than first-class in nature. Sadly, this undeniable greatness never occupied the national stage, the club's most significant events being three Metropolitan Opens, two Metropolitan Amateurs and a U.S. Open qualifier. Even more sadly, the once-impeccable finances of its founders could not save the course from being neglected during the Depression, causing it ultimately to be sold off to developers. Though a widely rumored removal of the seaside holes (presumably for real estate purposes) never took place, the Navy's occupation of the area during World War II led to the club's ultimate demise following the close of the 1942 season.

Today, the plot of land remains easily identifiable, with Macdonald's man-made lagoon retaining its shape and Lido Boulevard still curving its way through the heart of the property. A 1965 Robert Trent Jones municipal layout occupies the northern half of the site, but at the opposite end, tucked neatly into the southwest corner, remains the ever-glamorous Lido Club, its 400-plus rooms converted into modern condominiums. A far cry from C.B. Macdonald's vision, one assumes, but a marvelous reminder of the greatness which once was.

How the Lido Would Measure Up Today

As one of America's absolute best.

No doubt that its remarkably dovetailed routing could not have sustained even a yard's expansion, nor that the extreme proximity of holes would likely result in numerous lawsuits with modern equipment and higher volumes of play. But these points are trivial. The Lido was one of the greatest strategic golf courses ever built and, in a normal sea breeze, also one of the toughest. Restore the eighth to its original length and reduce the seventh (and perhaps the sixth) to par-4 status for tournament play and things would really have gotten difficult.

Every bit as good today as the day it was born.

Rising from the 1920s mist, the Lido Hotel is today the legendary facility's prime surviving feature. (*Golf Illustrated*)

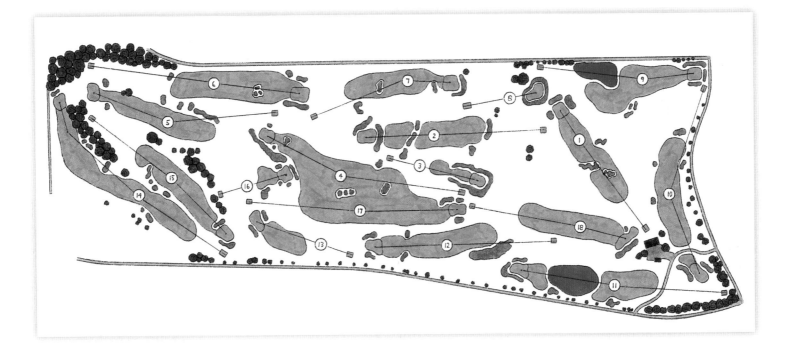

THE LINKS CLUB																				
309	388	201	455	400	453	318	150	333	3007	423	458	386	221	498	377	154	450	357	3324	6331
4	4	3	5	4	5	4	3	4	36	4	5	4	3	5	4	3	5	4	37	73

THE LINKS GOLF CLUB

ROSLYN, NY

Opened in 1919 / 6,331 yards Par-73

The Links Club, set on a small patch of Long Island real estate surrounded by properties belonging to such dignitaries as financier H.P. Whitney, Miami Beach developer Carl Fisher, and the family of Mr. W.R. Grace, was, to borrow a phrase from the political arena, a kinder and gentler Macdonald/Raynor design. Whereas its three predecessors in this book, Deepdale, Gibson Island, and The Lido, were planned on interesting sites with expectations of greatness, The Links was shoehorned into a tight, rectangular plot offering little in the way of outstanding contour or other natural features. Indeed, in later years it would be considered by some to be one of Long Island's easier courses, a place where short par-5s and only one par-4 in excess of 400 yards provided even the average player with a fair chance of turning in a decent score. But did Macdonald and Raynor intend it this way?

To answer this question, we must examine the club within the larger context of C.B. Macdonald's architectural career, specifically its spot as his first new project following completion of The Lido. This timing is important because while Seth Raynor began taking an active hand in Macdonald's design work as early as 1911, it was at The Lido in 1917 that his input may truly have begun to dominate the picture. Indeed following Raynor's untimely death in 1926, Macdonald suggested that The Lido would "stand forever as a monument to Mr. Raynor's constructive skill" and, as we have seen, even allowed the usage of "Raynor's Prized Dogleg" for the course's sixth hole.

In this context, the design of The Links Club was almost certainly Raynor's largest contribution to date, its squarish greens and pseudogeometric bunkering looking far more like his subsequent solo work than his execution of Macdonald's designs at The National or Deepdale. Would this explain the course's somewhat softer nature? A glance at Raynor's earliest solo projects, none of which would rank among his most demanding, suggests a cautiously optimistic "yes."

Such mysteries of genesis notwithstanding, it should be noted that The Links Club layout as we shall see it was a slightly altered version, owing to a set of modifications made by former Alister MacKenzie partner Perry Maxwell during the 1930s. These changes were not enormous in nature, generally amounting only to the addition of some fairly well-placed bunkers, but will be mentioned where they affected play materially. It should also be noted that the layout measured 6,178 yards in the early 1920s, but had been expanded to 6,331 by 1934.

Circa 1922 aerial (from a Bristol Steel Golf Shaft ad) shows original Macdonald/Raynor bunkering. Note the sharp elevation of the Biarritz green, upper right-center.
(*Golf Illustrated*)

Following a benign 309-yard opener, Raynor's design then moved swiftly into a set of four fine golf holes.

Number two, a 388-yard rendition of the Alps, was actually a somewhat modified version owing to what was more an elevated fairway than genuine Alp-like mounding short of the green.

The third was a 201-yard version of the Biarritz, its chief differences from the normal rendition being a single horseshoe bunker in place of the standard four and a green elevated rather highly, making for a particularly difficult long-iron approach.

At 455 yards, the fourth was a typically short par-5 of the period but played, as its name Hilltop suggested, to another elevated putting surface. Sharing an enormous double fairway with hole 17, it offered plenty of room off the tee, though the post-Raynor addition of two small bunkers short of the green presumably made one think a little longer before going for it in two.

The last of this stellar stretch was the 400-yard fifth, a long par-4 requiring an approach played over a fairly substantial valley. Originally the hole measured only 377 yards and featured none of the right-side fairway bunkering so prominent by the late '30s. In this instance, however, the new bunkering surely added interest to the drive, even if the primary hazard differed a bit from Raynor's more rectangular-oriented aesthetic.

Following a somewhat uninspired sixth and seventh, the outward half closed with the 150-yard Short eighth (played to a green considerably less round than the standard replica version) and the dual-option ninth, a pretty two-shotter wherein one played either boldly across a small pond or safely out to the right, the latter choice creating a far more awkward angle of approach.

Perhaps the most difficult hole on the back nine was the 221-yard reverse Redan 13th, one of the toughest-ever renditions of this most-copied creation. Originally only 204 yards, its subsequent lengthening may have stretched the limit of good balance for a hole generally built in the 180-190 yard range.

Another well-known replica came at the 154-yard Eden 16th, its front bunkers mirroring the Strath and Hill, with a rear trap approximating the dangers of the Eden estuary. Oddly, it appears that its angle of play may have been altered a bit over the years, the tee likely being moved to allow a lengthening of hole number 17.

Such an expansion was probably deemed necessary when the membership tired of playing their penultimate hole in its original form, as a 396-yard par-5. Though simply converting it to a par-4 was always an option, the club instead lengthened it to a more reasonable 450 yards, resulting in at least a marginal three-shotter heading back toward the clubhouse.

Despite measuring only 357 yards, the 18th was very much a suitable finisher, appearing to combine the finest elements of both the 17th and 18th greens at St. Andrew's. A slightly-elevated putting surface offered a Valley-of-Sin type run-up option while a front-left pot bunker, carved artfully into the putting surface, fairly approximated the danger of the infamous Road Hole original.

Clearly not an overpowering course then, The Links Club remained an extremely private, largely-unseen facility well into the mid 1980s. Eventually, a combination of rising taxes and membership policies so exclusive as to seriously deplete its numbers conspired to doom the property, and in 1985 it was finally sold off to developers for subdivision. Two hundred-plus private homes occupy the site today.

How the Links Would Measure Up Today

Like The Lido, the Links would not have lent itself well to significant rerouting or expansion. In fact, those early changes that were undertaken likely tapped out what little land may have been available for such purposes. Of course by now, holes four and seven would probably have been converted into par-4s, enhancing the course's challenge and perhaps giving it better balance in the process. Kinder and gentler? Definitely.

But a favorite of the tasteful connoisseur just the same.

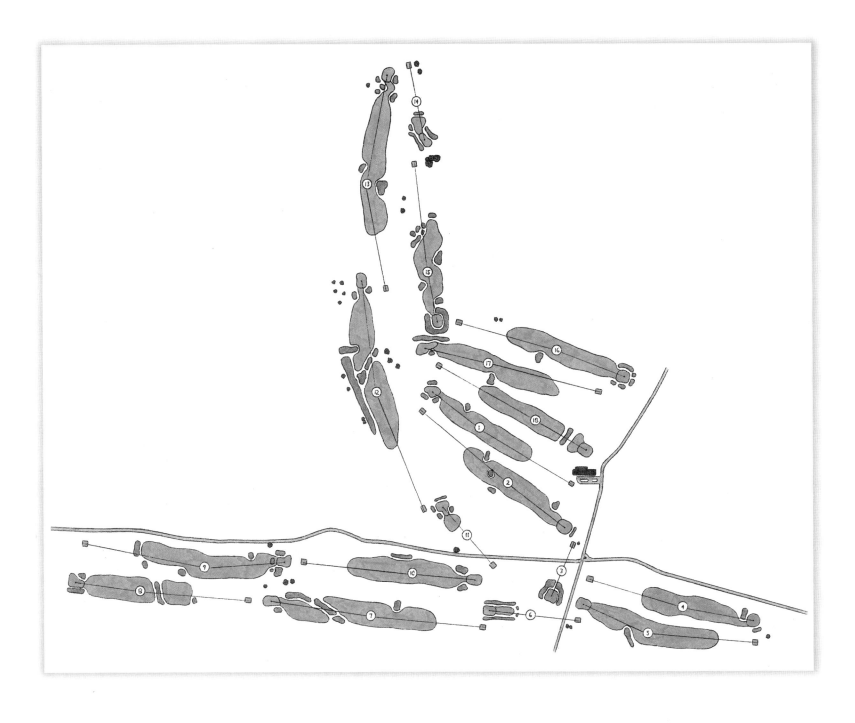

SHINNECOCK HILLS																			
353	400	120	356	381	200	461	317	430	3018	380	160	466	460	160	335	375	383	371	3090	6108
4	4	3	4	4	3	5	4	4	35	4	3	5	4	3	4	4	4	4	35	70

SHINNECOCK HILLS GOLF CLUB
SOUTHAMPTON, NY

Opened in 1916 / 6,108 yards Par-70

Shinnecock Hills has become justly famous in modern times, primarily as a now-regular U.S. Open venue, the trappings of which include a lofty perch among the highest reaches of most international course ratings. But while its nearly 70-year-old William Flynn-designed layout is unquestionably one of the best, the club also deserves recognition for a slightly less-obvious achievement: being that rare American facility to prosper in advance of, and without influence from, golf's stateside missionary, Charles Blair Macdonald. Shinnecock, in fact, predates all American clubs in the strictest sense for while it was not truly the first organized attempt at playing golf in the United States, it was, indisputably, the nation's first incorporated golfing entity.

Golf at Shinnecock Hills can be traced back to the season of 1891 when businessmen William Vanderbilt, Duncan Cryder, and Edward Mead, new converts to the game, commissioned Scotsman Willie Davis to build them a course at their Southampton summer retreat. Limited by financial constraints, Davis's effort amounted only to a rudimentary 12-holer, but its popularity led to the creation of a nine-hole women's course two years later. The men's course was expanded to 18 in 1895 (hosting both the U.S. Amateur and Open a year later) and likely underwent numerous smaller alterations in the years that followed. Finally in 1916, with advances in golf equipment and architecture rapidly making the Shinnecock links a relic, the decision was made to modernize the facility entirely.

Enter, of all people, Charles Blair Macdonald.

At the time of Shinnecock's founding, Macdonald had been an unknown Midwestern stockbroker. But now, some 25 years later, he represented golfing royalty. So much so, in fact, that by the time of his engagement by the club, he had already been given his famous architectural and financial carte blanche at The Lido, virtually guaranteeing that the concurrent Shinnecock project would enjoy neither his nor Raynor's highest attention. Perhaps it is not surprising, then, that the 6,108-yard layout they produced cannot be considered among their very finest, having more in common with, say, The Links Club than The Lido or Deepdale. Still, it was a course that featured many notable holes (both replicas and originals) and which at least partially occupied the same rolling land upon which the celebrated William Flynn design stands today.

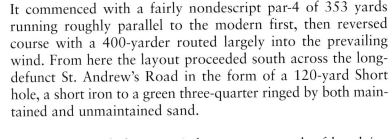

It commenced with a fairly nondescript par-4 of 353 yards running roughly parallel to the modern first, then reversed course with a 400-yarder routed largely into the prevailing wind. From here the layout proceeded south across the long-defunct St. Andrew's Road in the form of a 120-yard Short hole, a short iron to a green three-quarter ringed by both maintained and unmaintained sand.

The next seven holes occupied a narrow stretch of low-lying land pinched between the old Long Island Railroad line to the south and St. Andrew's Road to the north, a stretch that was probably the club's least exciting, yet hardly dismissable as mediocre. True one's pulse might not have quickened at the out-and-back fourth and fifth but the 200-yard Biarritz sixth was a legitimate attention-getter, and the reachable par-5 seventh and long par-4 ninth were also worthy of the critic's praise.

The 11th, a fine 160-yard version of the Eden, crossed back to the north side of St. Andrew's Road, finishing at a green positioned in the open area left of today's first hole.

Holes 13 and 14 in their original state (left) versus their configurations as numbers 3 and 7 today.

Next came the elaborately-bunkered 12th, a short par-5 played with the help of the prevailing breeze. While this hole did utilize some of the land employed in the present-day front-nine routing, it was entirely built over by Flynn and is in no way in play today. Macdonald and Raynor's 13th and 14th, however, were not so similarly obliterated.

Curiously, the 13th is seldom mentioned among the handful of fragments still remaining from the 1916 layout. But in addition to sharing the name Peconic, bestowed upon the present third hole, it ran an almost completely concurrent course. Though its tee was located a bit to the right of that used today, its greenside bunkers remain essentially intact (though the putting surface itself appears to have been moved back a bit) and the large right-side fairway trap is also still very much in play. So how tough was the Macdonald/Raynor version? At 460 downwind yards, it actually played seven yards *longer* than the present number three. It is not difficult to understand why the 14th hole was retained in its entirety (as the mod-

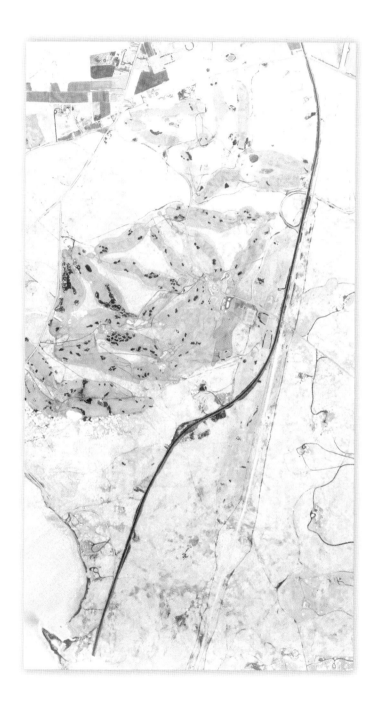

Remains of many Macdonald/Raynor holes are still visible in this 1938 aerial survey. Note the Biarritz and Short holes adjacent to the rail line, with Eden just to their left. (National Archives)

ern seventh) for it is, by nearly universal acclaim, among the finest Redans ever built. A new tee has lengthened it from 160 to 188 yards and some of the bunker shaping has evolved over the years but the essential Redan challenge—green falling away back-left, deep bunker fronting it—remains timeless.

The 335-yard Cape 15th continued directly into the wind, playing to one of the very few Shinnecock greens bunkered with Raynor's trademark severity. Like the Lido's Cape fifth, this version did not feature the dogleg configuration of Macdonald's more famous renditions at The National and Mid Ocean, but it did provide some second-shot advantage for the player who successfully carried the menacing right-side fairway bunkers.

The closers traversed back and forth beneath the famous elevated clubhouse with the most recognizable being the Road 17th, a nearly straightaway version lacking any right-side hazard to approximate the old railway sheds of St. Andrew's.

Finally the 18th, though only 375 yards in length, may well have been the toughest hole on the golf course, owing mostly to the fact that it played to the same elevated greensite still vexing golfers at the ninth hole today. This putting surface, carved from a fairly steep hillside, was completely fronted by one very deep cross-bunker, making for an extremely challenging second, particularly into the prevailing wind.

The Macdonald/Raynor course at Shinnecock Hills was among their shortest-lived, remaining in play only until 1930. At this time, the State of New York opted to extend Route 27, the primary east-west corridor of Long Island's South Shore, directly across the southern part of the property, rendering several of the lower-lying holes unusable. With Raynor deceased and Macdonald retired, the club passed on Charles Banks and turned instead to William Flynn for their reconfiguration, providing him with the additional acreage upon which 10 of today's present 18 holes currently sit. Notably, 11 of the Macdonald/Raynor hole names were retained, though only one (both openers being called Westward Ho!) remains in its original sequence.

How Shinnecock Hills Would Measure Up Today

Not exceptionally well.

Even without the Route 27 expansion, this relatively short layout would have struggled to hold a noteworthy position in the modern age. For while room did exist to lengthen many holes (particularly those situated north of St. Andrew's Road), the overall degree of challenge, particularly within the green complexes, was not as consistently high as at many other Macdonald/Raynor courses. Consequently, this at best would have ended up as something of a cult favorite, hardly a U.S. Open site but an engaging track filled with character and interesting shots. Most lost courses turn into housing developments but at Shinnecock Hills, unwelcomed change led to the construction of William Flynn's timeless classic. Wanted or not, one senses that the club did pretty well in that deal.

ALSO BY CHARLES BLAIR MACDONALD

Although some controversy remains, a strong argument can be made that C.B. Macdonald's second Chicago Golf Club design, built in Wheaton in 1895, was in fact America's first 18-hole golf course. Macdonald himself muddied the issue by suggesting that his first Chicago course, the 1892 nine-holer in Belmont, had already expanded by this time, but local period newspaper articles discount this pointedly. Should such press reports be wrong, however, the Wheaton boosters can still take heart, for theirs was surely the oldest *lost* 18-holer in America, hands down.

And yet many tend to overlook this fact, perhaps unaware of the magnitude of Seth Raynor's 1923 "renovation" which, for all intents and purposes, laid to rest any remnants of Macdonald's historic Wheaton original.

As the adjacent map suggests, the stories of C.B.'s self-oriented design style were entirely true as evidenced by the old course's routing running clockwise to keep his trademark slice comfortably in-bounds. It is also worth noting that while Macdonald generally drew influence from the classic British links, his Chicago design offered no real replica holes. Additionally, it had been stretched more than 700 yards by the time of its remodeling, the inevitable by-product of hosting three U.S. Opens and four U.S. Amateurs prior to 1913.

While the Macdonald/Raynor team did build several poorly documented private estate courses, their lone additional loss of significance was the Number Three Course at West Virginia's famous Greenbrier Resort, a layout occupying much of the same land covered by Jack Nicklaus's Greenbrier Course today. Though heavily altered long before Jack's arrival, the old layout (apparently built mostly by Raynor) measured 6,344 yards at the time of its 1924 opening, playing to a rather demanding par of 70. It too featured the standard replicas, which proved to be something of a novelty years later when resort scorecards continued to use names like Cape, Eden, Short and Biarritz to describe holes bearing no resemblance whatsoever to those much-emulated classics.

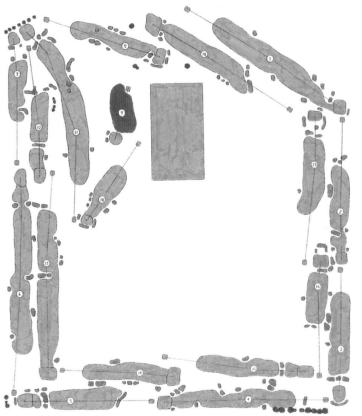

Chicago GC's original C.B. Macdonald layout, circa 1920.

CHICAGO																				
460	363	333	418	333	566	317	300	130	3220	241	504	326	520	300	374	315	383	420	3383	6603
5	4	4	4	4	5	4	4	3	37	4	5	4	5	4	4	4	4	4	38	75

A classic short green at the Greenbrier.
Note the horseshoe-shaped ridge within the
putting surface. (*Golf Illustrated*)

It can fairly be said that no architect has lost a greater core of golf courses—the very heart of his work, really—than Charles Blair Macdonald. Thankfully, while these historic designs are but a memory, The National Golf Links of America, where it really all began, still remains, a suitable monument to a monumental talent.

DR. ALISTER MACKENZIE

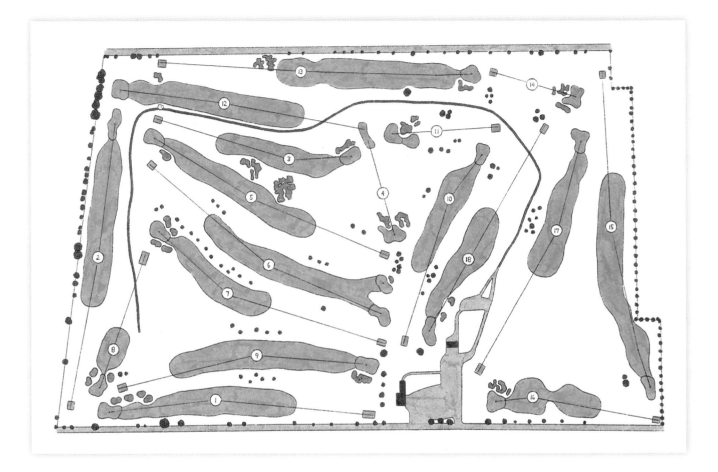

BAYSIDE																				
440	460	305	160	430	450	420	225	425	3315	350	180	405	490	150	505	290	410	390	3170	6485
4	5	4	3	4	4	4	3	4	35	4	3	4	5	3	5	4	4	4	36	71

BAYSIDE GOLF LINKS
BAYSIDE, NY

Opened in 1932 / 6,485 yards Par-71

Though American golf is, was, and likely always will be, a game best-suited for the affluent, its roots in Great Britain were considerably more egalitarian in nature. Many of the game's early links occupied common land, of course, and its cost was, to say the least, a bit less prohibitive than today's world of "upscale daily fees" and "quality golf."

With such an everyman's mentality at its traditional core, it is hardly surprising that so many of the game's great architects—themselves a decidedly British lot—spoke eloquently of municipal golf and its importance to the sport's long-term well-being. Interestingly, such well-born American designers as A.W. Tillinghast and George Thomas were equally staunch public course advocates, with Thomas going so far as to finance the completion of Los Angeles's Griffith Park layouts out of his own pocket.

While that particular degree of commitment might be difficult to outdo, few of the great architects addressed the public golf cause more directly than the legendary Scotsman, Dr. Alister MacKenzie, who wrote:

"I hope to live to see the day when there are the crowds of municipal courses, as in Scotland, cropping up all over the world. It would help enormously in increasing the health, the virility and the prosperity of nations, and would do much to counteract discontent and Bolshevism. There can be no possible reason against and there is every reason in favor of, municipal courses."

Though this paragraph's political reference was surely a serious one, MacKenzie was in fact a bit of a character, a bona fide M.D. holding degrees in both chemistry and natural science who served in the British army during the Boer War. A marketing man's dream with his Scottish accent, plus-fours and fondness for the bottle, MacKenzie cut his teeth as a partner with H.S. Colt and his long-term associate C.H. Alison, then enhanced his name recognition dramatically by winning the 1914 *Country Life* magazine contest for the best design of a hypothetical par-4.

Having already gone solo several years previously, MacKenzie emigrated to the United States in the mid-1920s. There he quickly completed such enduring classics as Cypress Point, Crystal Downs, and Pasatiempo, fully establishing his celebrity prior to the onset of the Depression at decade's end.

Given the economic upheaval that followed, it is perhaps more than coincidence that the Good Doctor finally built the fine public courses he so obviously favored in the early 1930s. With most private financing rendered impotent, only municipalities (with their steady tax bases) and men shrewd enough to recognize the cash-flow possibilities of public golf were actively engaged in course construction. Thus in the midst of the Depression, while many architects suffered, Alister MacKenzie managed to complete his bicoastal public gems, the Bayside Links in New York and suburban San Francisco's Sharp Park.

Among architectural fans, few lost courses have provoked as much interest as Bayside, due mostly, one assumes, to the uniformly high level of MacKenzie's other work. Was it in fact a layout worthy of such expectation? Objectively speaking, probably not. Limited to a relatively small tract of rather average land, its routing had a bit of the banal back-and-forth about it, and the course generally lacked the sort of spectacular feature holes and wildly-inspiring aesthetic one expects from a topflight MacKenzie design.

What Bayside possessed in spades, however, were two of MacKenzie's other vintage traits: character, and a degree of difficulty in apparent excess of its relatively modest length. The latter is not hard to account for as the Doctor's fondness for shorter par-4s (Bayside featured two-shotters measuring 290 and 305 yards) provided ample room for a number of offsetting longer ones, in this case a robust seven measuring in excess of 400 yards. As far as the character issue goes, one can chalk this up to both extraordinary contouring of the green complexes and, perhaps, a sense of the artistic so frequently lacking in today's design world. The result of this powerful combination was an approximation of a British links so fine that an early promotional flier quoted the great Walter Hagen as saying:

"Bayside is truly British in character and super-British in condition. I'll practice there for the British Open."

Words to make a Scottish doctor proud.

From all appearances, Bayside's front nine was the more difficult half, measuring 145 yards longer than the back while playing to a *lower* par of 35. As if to demonstrate this challenge,

1942 aerial survey appears to reveal not only the Bayside layout
but some of the land's contour as well. (National Archives)

the opener was a 440-yard par-4, a stiff test at any juncture but especially difficult right out of the gate. Menaced right by bunkers and left by Little Bayside Road, it was a hole where all but the best were likely satisfied with a chip and two putts for five.

The short par-5 second and well-bunkered third provided some letup and the 160-yard fourth, vaguely reminiscent of the longer fourth at Augusta National, featured one of golf's more imaginatively shaped greens. These fairly manageable holes completed, however, a purely man-sized test of shotmaking remained for the duration of the front nine.

This bruising stretch began with the 430-yard fifth, a hole whose driving area was sandwiched between a wild, rough-edged bunker typical of the MacKenzie style and a series of grass ridges. Once in the fairway, the player faced a slightly uphill second to a green set between a series of large mounds right and a steep fallaway to the left.

Reversing course 180 degrees, the 450-yard sixth was the longest par-4 at Bayside and possibly its most difficult, with more undulation making a level fairway lie a rarity and its small green virtually surrounded by additional mounding. Curiously, the sixth also included an alternate green, a far-left putting surface which was regularly played, though for what reason we do not know.

The 420-yard seventh was similarly brawny, yet for the man grown weary of lengthy par-4s, the one-shot eighth represented only a faint breather. At 225 yards, it generally required a full-blooded wood just to bring the green into range and while MacKenzie did leave room for shots to be run onto the putting surface, two ample mounds positioned some 20 yards short had to be carried for such to truly become feasible.

The 425-yard ninth closed the outward half fittingly but it wasn't long before things returned to a more classical aura at the 180-yard 11th, a hole which appears from detailed scorecard drawings to have been a reverse Redan. Though hardly the fan of replica holes that the Macdonald/Raynor camp was, MacKenzie would later sing the praises of the Redan upon building a wonderful version (since altered) with Bobby Jones on the sixth at Augusta National. At Bayside the lay of the land dictated a green sloping from front-left to back-right and there were no rear bunkers, but the resemblance and intent seem apparent.

Following the 405-yard 12th, the 490-yard 13th was a simple, yet strategically sound par-5 that was potentially reachable in two. The catch: regardless of whether one was going for it or laying up, a greenside bunker dictated the best angle of approach to be from the left— the side menaced prominently by two fairway traps and out-of-bounds for its duration.

The 505-yard, hazardless 15th was an equally tempting par-5, its crowned fairway providing an excellent vantage point from which to attack the small green guarded only by a nearby out-of-bounds fence.

Now hemmed tightly into a corner, MacKenzie utilized what little land remained to make number 16 a fascinating short par-4. Measuring only 290 yards, it ran along the property's northwest boundary to a green guarded front-right by sand and left by Little Bayside Road, offering the player three distinct options. For the faint of heart, lots of fairway was provided to the right, making for an easy drive but a difficult approach over the greenside bunkers. A more aggressive drive along the boundary line had to carry a cluster of mounds roughly 200 yards out but opened an unobscured line for one's second. Or, for the behemoth among us, there was always the chance to throw caution to the wind and aim directly for the putting surface.

Unlike many of his contemporaries, Dr. MacKenzie was not wedded to the concept of making his finisher a par-4 of enormous proportion, as his 18th holes at Cypress Point (346 yards), Crystal Downs (400), and Pastiempo (a 173-yard par-3) richly illustrate. At Bayside he created a relatively straightforward 390-yarder played to a long, narrow green fronted left by sand and right, for one final time, by significant mounding.

All told, was Bayside worthy of the curiosity that has surrounded it for lo these many years? As a course to be compared with MacKenzie's best work, probably not. As a study in what can be done on a limited site with little more than the architect's native creativity, very much so. And as a public facility located in the heart of the nation's largest urban area, absolutely—for Bayside was infinitely better than any public course still in play in New York or, arguably, most any other major American city.

Naturally the Suburban Manifest Destiny that buried the borough of Queens with New York-style overdevelopment eventually caught up to Bayside and the property was sold off for housing during the 1950s. As a handful of intrepid historians and researchers have discovered upon checking, any connection between it and the present-day Kissena Park municipal course nearby is strictly imaginary, as not a trace of Dr. MacKenzie's sole New York-area original exists today.

How Bayside Would Measure Up Today

As a great public golf course, the sometimes-severe contouring of whose green complexes would draw constant attention.

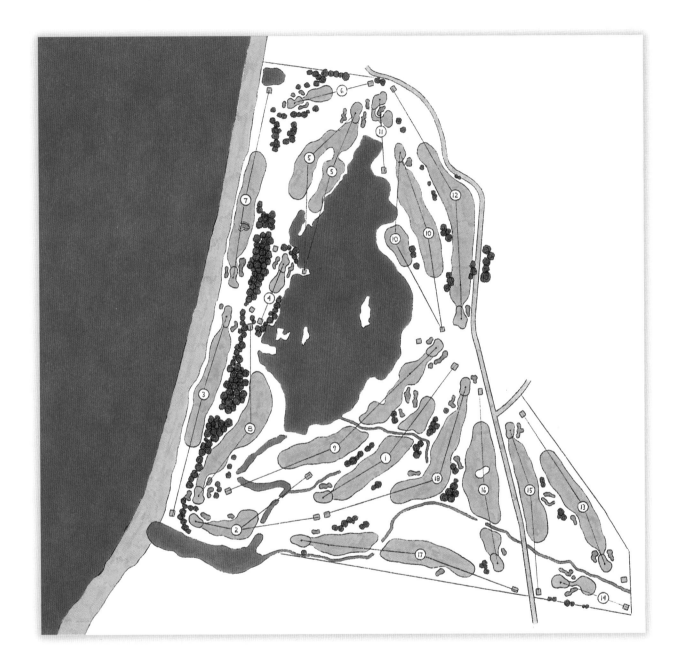

SHARP PARK																				
400	274	423	120	338	168	383	398	538	3042	392	142	483	345	143	330	363	471	443	3112	6154
4	4	4	3	4	3	4	4	5	35	4	3	5	4	3	4	4	5	4	36	71

SHARP PARK GOLF COURSE
PACIFICA, CA

Opened in 1931 / 6,154 yards Par-71

As today, some 65 years after his death, Dr. Alister MacKenzie remains perhaps the most celebrated golf architect in history, it is truly remarkable that two public courses he laid out in major American metropolises could have been so short-lived and poorly documented. Yet Bayside, as we have seen, labored in (and vanished into) almost complete obscurity—and it cannot even begin to compare with the briefly-lived legacy of San Francisco's Sharp Park.

MacKenzie's Sharp Park layout is surely one of golf architecture's most enduring mysteries. Owing to the fact that it was built in 1931, then washed into oblivion by a coastal storm shortly thereafter, its original design was seen firsthand by very few. Nor was this initial version in any way adequately recorded, with few photographs of any kind known to remain in existence. Further, a visit to today's 6,299-yard facility offers little; this vastly-altered layout serving mostly to make one wonder if a vintage MacKenzie design ever *could* have existed upon this site.

But the Doctor's original, located very much upon this same land, was all that its tantalizing prospects have suggested, a marvelous golf course featuring seaside holes, two double fairways, a large lake, and a cypress-dotted setting fairly reminiscent of Monterey. It was, in short, a municipal masterpiece.

Located just 10 miles south of downtown San Francisco, the site given to MacKenzie was uncommonly fine for a public facility, including a nearly 1,000-yard oceanfront stretch along Salada Beach. For a county whose public course facilities at Harding and Lincoln Parks were among the busiest in the nation, the development of Sharp Park was a godsend, but this wonderful property was not without its drawbacks.

For one thing, a fair amount of the land required shoring up with massive quantities of dredged sand in an expensive, Lido-like operation. Second, the site was partially divided by a small county road, a circumstance dictating that three of MacKenzie's back-nine holes be separated from their 15 brethen. Years later this road would be rerouted, though by that time the storm-driven reconfiguration of the golf course would still leave four newer holes separated, about the only commonality between MacKenzie's work and the course in play today.

The 1931 layout began with a dogleg-right par-4 of 400 yards, a strong but not especially memorable opener. But things changed quickly at the second, a 274-yard par-4 with alternate tees situated on either side of the first green. In what today might be referred to as "risk/reward" style, this nearly-driveable hole featured a large bunker front-right of the putting surface and a lake to the left of the fairway, creating the wonderful question of just how near the water one dared to venture in pursuit of an easier angle for his second.

The third was a long two-shotter of 423 yards, playing directly north along the beachfront. Again the risk/reward question was laid before us: play safely down the middle and deal with a front-right greenside bunker or aggressively skirt the beach in pursuit of an open second? Seaside winds generally affected play at Sharp Park greatly, bringing those most unlinkish of obstacles—trees—into play along the right side as well.

Following the short fourth, a precise pitch played along the lake's westward shoreline, one reached the first of the dual-fairway holes, the 338-yard fifth. Here the player's options were numerous with a "safe" left-side route leaving the most difficult second-shot, a dangerous lakefront fairway opening up a more direct line, or the all-out blast over everything leaving a mere pitch from a wide-open angle. As at the second hole, a second tee positioned left of the previous green served to create additional angles and variety.

The 385-yard seventh was the course's second and last seaside hole, playing directly south to a long, narrow green flanked on either side by sand. The slight angling of the putting surface again tempted one to drive close to the beach (particularly if the pin was cut back-left), but the lesser presence of trees at least made this tee shot a bit more forgiving.

The 398-yard eighth, though built with only one fairway, offered two very distinct lines of play. A drive aimed safely left was simple enough but set up a nearly all-carry approach across two front-left greenside bunkers. For the man capable of controlling a long fade, however, there was the option of skirting the treeline, a shot which, if brought off successfully, again yielded a more favorable approach.

Though one hesitates to name a best hole among so many good ones, the 392-yard 10th did

1943 aerial survey reveals a number of MacKenzie's original holes still
intact, plus four newer ones built to the east. (National Archives)

a fine job of nominating itself. Here was the double fairway concept played out to the fullest, the right side providing ample safety but a bunker-obscured second, the left requiring a gutsy tee shot to a water-guarded fairway but yielding a straight-on approach. Yet again, dual tee boxes varied the challenge from day to day, making the 10th a truly great hole—but an intimidating prospect for anyone hoping to slip past the starter and begin play on the back nine.

Following the 142-yard 11th came the long 12th, a 493-yarder distinctly reachable in two, provided one avoided several prominent trees and the out-of-bounds which ran down the entire left side.

Perhaps not surprisingly, the three holes exiled across the county road were not among the layout's finest, the 345-yard 13th being the best of the bunch with out-of-bounds also threatening its more-favored left side.

With the routing having returned to the clubhouse for a third time, one set out again at the 363-yard 16th, a par-4 following much the same path as today's first hole. Here a large mound punctuated the fairway some 175 yards off the tee, offering several different angles of play. The more difficult drive was the one aimed down the right side, close to a clump of trees. Naturally this choice also provided the better approach angle to a deep, narrow putting surface.

MacKenzie closed out Sharp Park with a pair of long finishers beginning with the 471-yard 17th. Though not a particularly difficult hole, this short par-5 often faced a strong sea breeze and featured out-of-bounds left, two bunkers, a meandering brook and a green laid precariously close to a rough, marshy depression. The 18th, by contrast, was a bit of a monster, its 443 yards requiring more brute strength than finesse, though the ability to draw one's tee shot would obviously have come in handy.

It was indeed unfortunate for Sharp Park that so many of its best holes fell along the property's ocean side, for it was this flank which took the brunt of any incoming storms. Following the early 1930s deluge that washed several of these gems out to sea, a massive berm was constructed (largely upon land once occupied by holes three and seven) to prevent history from repeating itself. The subsequent rerouting of the county road and reconfiguring of the lakeside holes has further muddled things so that today only a handful of holes run consistent with MacKenzie's originals, and no appreciable trace of his strategy remains in play.

How Sharp Park Would Measure Up Today

Oceanfront holes, double fairways, MacKenzie bunkering, marvelous scenery...

Any way you look at it, even at only 6,154 yards, Sharp Park would have to stand well out in front as America's finest municipal golf course.

Restoration anyone?

SETH RAYNOR

OAKLAND																			
412	150	435	320	300	445	385	155	408	3070	315	325	425	190	220	430	350	415	445	3115	6185
4	3	4	4	4	5	4	3	4	35	4	4	4	3	3	4	4	4	5	35	70

OAKLAND GOLF CLUB

BAYSIDE, NY

Opened in 1915 / 6,185 yards Par-70

For the familiar eye, just one look at the accompanying aerial photograph of the Oakland Golf Club will be enough to recognize the architectural handiwork of Seth Raynor. The squarish greens, the Biarritz and Redan replicas, the almost geometrically positioned bunkers...these and several other idiosyncratic trademarks tended to appear in the vast majority of Raynor's work, making him at once one of the most talented and curious designers that the field of golf course architecture has ever seen.

Yet long before Raynor had even been introduced to the royal and ancient game, there was already an Oakland Golf Club. One of America's oldest organized clubs, Oakland traced its roots back as far as 1896 when a gentleman named John H. Taylor leased 111 acres of a Bayside estate called The Oaks and hired Scotsman Tom Bendelow to build a nine-hole layout. Truly at the cutting edge of golf's growth in America, Taylor's club included numerous charter members who knew little of the game but wanted to learn, among them a future three-time U.S. Amateur champion named Walter Travis. Travis, in fact, played his first round of golf on the original Oakland course at the ripe old age of thirty-five, likely marking the latest launching of a championship golf career on record.

The Oakland course was extremely popular in its early years, with a volume of play great enough to merit an expansion to 18 holes in 1906. Counting Vanderbilts, Whitneys, and several prominent politicians among its membership, the club was the site of numerous regional tournaments, entertaining most of the day's top professionals in the process. Widely praised despite its hilly terrain, Oakland also became one of the earliest examples of a Green Committee run amok when, about 1913, a large number of ugly and ill-positioned bunkers were inexplicably added. It was not long after this time, reports of the desecration becoming common, that Seth Raynor was called onto the scene.

Raynor, of course, had by now cut his teeth with Charles Blair Macdonald and was just beginning to make a name for himself as a solo designer. Indeed, at roughly the same time that he was reworking Oakland, he was also producing his first original layout at the Westhampton Country Club, as well as 18 more for another Long Island club, Bellport. But among these efforts Oakland was clearly the most interesting. For it was here that his work most obviously resembled so many of his subsequent "co-designs" with Macdonald, providing real ammunition for those who suggest that C.B. was frequently but a ceremonial partner.

Whatever the case, it can safely be said that Raynor's course at Oakland was among his most underrated designs. For while it may not have equaled such classics as Fishers Island, Camargo, and Shoreacres, it was one of the finest in New York City at a time when such implied more than simply having grass on one's greens and an average playing time of less than six hours. It was, all told, a most interesting and occasionally spectacular layout.

Aerial photo, circa 1925. Note both the still-rural nature of Bayside, Queens and the original Raynor bunkering, some of which had evolved by the onset of World War II (as mapped). (*Golf Illustrated*)

Unlike some Raynor tracks, Oakland began in particularly taxing fashion with a 412-yard par-4, a hole which swooped down from the elevated clubhouse, rambled past an enormous right-side bunker and across the entrance road, then continued uphill to a large green guarded by five additional bunkers.

The second was likely the club's easiest hole but the breather was short-lived, as the 435-yard third ranked firmly among its very toughest. Here Raynor clearly designed things to challenge both the pro and duffer equally, placing right-side bunkers in the landing areas of the weaker man's first two shots but also building a large, intimidating hazard along the preferred left side of the scratch man's driving area.

Number one tee, 1922. (*The American Golfer*)

Following the short but dangerous fourth and the 360-yard fifth (likely a small-scale Alps), one reached the excellent but diminutive par-5 sixth, a brief 445-yarder which tempted the good player to go for the green in two, provided he was prepared to carry the narrow ravine which crossed well in front of it.

The ravine figured even more prominently at the 385-yard seventh, arguably the club's most memorable hole and one which stands up well on any list of all-time lost classics. Though not terribly long, it required forced carries of the abyss on both the drive and approach, leaving little margin for error on either. Inexplicably rated as only the number 11 stroke hole on early scorecards, it is believed to have occupied much of the same land as Bendelow's "Heavenly Twins," a notoriously difficult hole dating back to before the turn of the century.

The ravine also came into play at the 155-yard eighth, another forced carry and possibly a loose adaptation of the Short hole. Like number seven, the eighth represented an early version of target golf, with few palatable alternatives to placing one's tee shot squarely upon the putting surface. The 400-yard ninth, on the other hand, provided a bit more room to operate, though a single bunker carved flush in the heart of the driving area made for a tricky finish to an impressive front nine.

Slightly less demanding out of the gate, the inward half began with a not-quite-easy 315-yard par-4, a 90-degree dogleg requiring a short pitch to a putting surface all but encircled by sand. Though driving the green might well have been an option for the longer hitter, the odd angle of approach combined with the possibility of landing upon a paved access road and careening halfway to Southampton likely tempered many such thoughts.

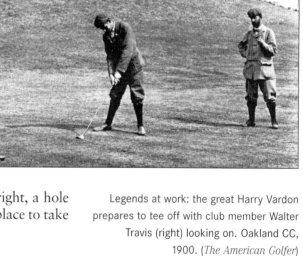

Oakland entered its second four-hole stretch of distinction at the 425-yard 12th, a difficult two-shotter played to the sort of nearly square putting surface that Raynor so favored.

The 190-yard 13th and 220-yard 14th were the obligatory Redan and Biarritz, oddly positioned back-to-back (a one-time occurrence in the Raynor portfolio) and every bit as challenging as one might expect of these perennial favorites.

And finally there came the 430-yard 15th, the second longest par-4 on the golf course and, with 10 bunkers in play and a paved road to the right, a hole offering little in the way of leniency. Like most of Oakland's two-shotters, a good place to take one's four and go quietly.

Legends at work: the great Harry Vardon prepares to tee off with club member Walter Travis (right) looking on. Oakland CC, 1900. (*The American Golfer*)

The routing of the club's finishing stretch was rather curious, likely having been mandated both by the often-demanding terrain and the remnants of several roads which wandered about the old Oaks estate. Though all three holes stood up well, the 350-yard 16th was a bit different in its configuration, running northward along the edge of a tree-lined road, then elbowing somewhat awkwardly to a green strangely devoid of bunkering in front or to the sides. Resembling no other Raynor design of record, it also utilized the quirky and not-altogether-fair interior out-of-bounds rule, deeming any ball that crossed the pavement left of the fairway subject to penalty.

The 17th, on the other hand, was a much more straightforward hole, running southward across the entry road past a very large cross-bunker to a green shaded amid a row of oak trees. Reversing course 180 degrees, the 445-yard 18th was an eminently reachable par-5, its uphill finish culminating in a green situated directly before the clubhouse, allowing for sizable audiences to observe the completion of play.

Like most private courses located within New York City's five boroughs, Oakland faced growing post-World War II pressure from suburban expansion. Unlike such neighbors as Bayside, Pomonok, and Fresh Meadow, however, it fell victim not to real estate developers but to New York State construction, first of the Long Island Expressway in 1952, then the Clearview Expressway in 1960. With Queensboro Community College occupying some of the former property, the clubhouse served as the school's administration building for a time, but little trace of this historic club and its wonderful golf course remains today.

How Oakland Would Measure Up Today

The problem here would be exclusively one of distance, particularly with no hole longer than 445 yards and par already being 70. One modernizing possibility might have been to stretch the sixth (a true thinking man's par-5), convert the 425-yard 12th into a short three-shotter and let number 18 stand unaltered as a testing 445-yard par-4 closer. Such would still leave Oakland a tad short for modern competition—but you'd seldom see it torn up in everyday play.

ALSO BY SETH RAYNOR

Much space within this book has been dedicated to the question of who actually built many of the courses sharing the label "Macdonald & Raynor," the result being precious few lost designs clearly attributable solely to Seth Raynor.

One important former course that does appear to qualify is the legendary Ocean Links, a remarkable nine-holer built on the Newport, Rhode Island, estate of New York banker and sportsman T. Suffern Tailer. Situated between the famous Newport Country Club and the nearby waters of the Atlantic Ocean, Raynor's creation featured the usual mix of replica holes (a fine Redan third, a Short sixth, and a Road eighth), plus several holes mixing both original and borrowed playing characteristics. Its closer, a fantastically difficult 460-yard par-4 was a replica of Raynor's own "Prize Dogleg," a hole originally debuted (as a par-5) as the sixth hole at The Lido.

In addition to being a fine golf course, Ocean Links's fame was in part due to hosting Mr. Tailer's annual Gold Mashie tournament, an invitational featuring many of the day's best professionals competing over 72 holes for the Gold Mashie Trophy. Opened for play in 1920, Ocean Links was yet another beauty whose life proved all too brief, being sold off by Tailer's Depression-needy widow in 1931.

Ocean Links third green, another classic Macdonald/Raynor Redan. The player with hands on hips (at left) is T. Suffern Tailer, the course's owner. (*Golf Illustrated*)

Another highly-private facility was the nine-hole Babson Park Golf and Yacht Club, located just a few minutes southeast of Lake Wales, Florida. This 3,240-yard, par-35 layout was apparently built for an affluent gentleman who had been involved with Raynor's nearby Mountain Lake development but desired his own personal playground as well. An interesting footnote: period guidebooks listed the club as being reachable by boat, though with its water access limited to nearby Lake Caloosa, one wonders just how many visitors that option might have applied to.

Though evidence occasionally pops up suggesting the one-time existence of several other Raynor solo layouts, little is recorded of their specifics, perhaps due to the designer's penchant for working with the wealthiest of American society and the high degree of privacy associated therewith.

Donald Ross

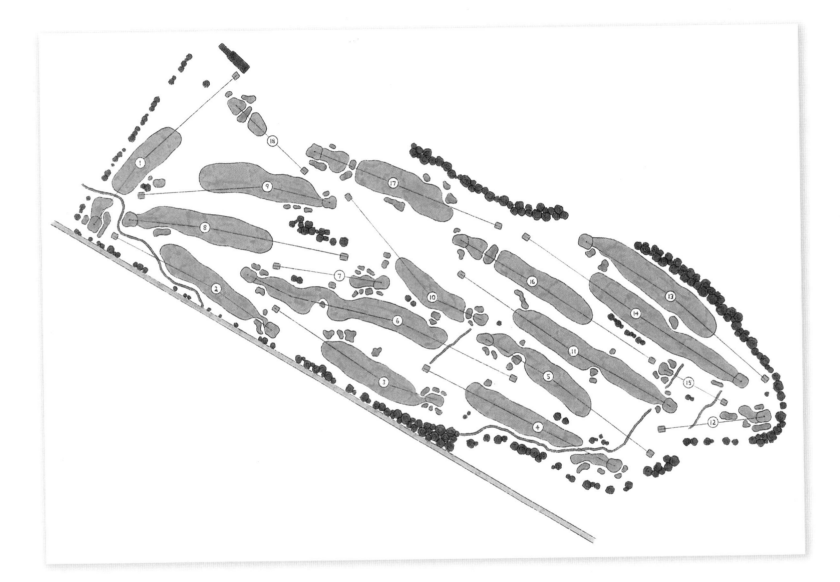

ENGLEWOOD																				
373	355	345	378	377	510	190	392	354	3274	332	450	192	405	469	122	398	405	165	2938	6212
4	4	4	4	4	5	3	4	4	36	4	5	3	4	5	3	4	4	3	35	71

ENGLEWOOD COUNTRY CLUB
ENGLEWOOD, NJ

Remodeled in 1916 / 6,212 yards Par-71

Though having Donald Ross's name attached to a course generally assures a high degree of respect in the world of golf, the Englewood Country Club represented something of an odd exception: a place that enjoyed its rather prominent peak of fortune well before the legendary Scottish architect ever set foot on the property.

Located slightly inland from the New Jersey entrance to the George Washington Bridge, the club's golfing history dated back to 1896 when an intrepid group of members laid out a rather rudimentary nine-hole course measuring roughly 2,520 yards, with a par of 35. In 1900, with the game's growing popularity causing overcrowding, this facility was expanded to 18, though no record exists as to precisely who was responsible for the renovation.

Lacking such records, little additional information exists to document this early layout, save its length (6,205 yards in 1909) and par (71). We can assume, however, that it must have been a pretty fair track, for in 1906 it was selected to host the U.S. Amateur, at that time America's most important golf championship.

Due to the success of the Amateur (won by Eben Byers of Pittsburgh), Englewood was soon awarded the 1909 U.S. Open, a tournament captured by British professional George Sargent with a then-record, four-round total of 291. Another scoring milestone was achieved during this event when contestants Tom McNamara and David Hunter became the first men to break 70 in National Open play, recording 69 and 68 respectively. Not surprisingly, the common description of the course following the championship was "moderately easy," the lone possible dissenter being prominent British professional Tom Vardon who topped a drive into the brook at the par-4 second and proceeded to rack up an attention-grabbing eight!

But the idea that Englewood might be a bit soft for the big boys was now widely accepted, and hosting the 1911 Metropolitan Open did little to stem the tide. On this occasion, Gilbert Nichols compiled an all-time 72-hole record score of 281, nearly setting the place on fire with a torrid final-round 66. Clearly, if Englewood wished to remain a viable tournament venue, some significant change was needed.

The par-three seventh at Englewood, Walter Hagen putting. (*Golf Illustrated*)

A comparison of before and after scorecards suggests that while Donald Ross's 1916 alterations may have been substantial, they likely did not involve a wholesale reworking of the original routing. Still, significant new bunkering and green contouring were very much in evidence, leaving little doubt that the post-Ross layout was far, far better than its predecessor. And thus brought fully up to modern speed, Englewood proceeded to defy all odds by never again being selected to host a nationally-important golf championship.

Reasons? The compact property's lack of gallery space perhaps, or the fact that the rapid development of newer courses on the New York side of the Hudson provided the Metropolitan Golf Association with logistically better options in those pre-George Washington Bridge days. But a more direct answer likely lay in the renovation's general timing, for this was the beginning of golf design's Golden Age, a period in which the development of literally dozens of outstanding courses nationwide began to push such time-honored tournament venues as Newport, the Myopia Hunt Club, and Englewood to the sidelines. Indeed, during the decade of the 1920s, the U.S. Open visited 10 first-time sites, an occurrence which had never taken place previously, nor since.

Englewood member Oswald Kirkby tees off at number eight en route to the 1914 Metropolitan Open championship. Note the old-style "chocolate drop" mounds of the pre-Donald Ross layout. (*Golf Illustrated*)

Regardless, Ross's Englewood redesign really was a good one, providing the club with a short but highly engaging test upon which a wandering brook came into play on at least eight occasions.

In an odd quirk of design, the layout began with a run of five consecutive mid-length par-4s, all ranging between 345 and 373 yards. Of this group the 355-yard second seems to have drawn the most attention (particularly from the ill-fated Tom Vardon), though the heavily bunkered 378-yard fourth probably was the most difficult.

The par-5 sixth, at 510 yards, was by far Englewood's longest hole, a nearly straightaway affair tempting the big hitter to have a go at it in two. The 190-yard bunker-lined seventh was certainly no pushover and the 392-yard eighth, its green backed up flush against the brook, obviously required a delicate approach.

Though slightly shorter overall, the back nine was probably Englewood's better half in that it featured some longer par-4s and a triplet of varied and interesting one-shotters. The longest of these was the 192-yard 12th but the best may have been the 122-yard 15th, comfortably the club's shortest hole but one played to a narrow green bunkered on either side and fronted by the outermost reaches of the brook. Then, after two full-size par-4s, came the 165-yard 18th, a hole requiring only modest length but considerable accuracy, its putting surface flanked on three sides by sand and on the fourth by a steep embankment.

Aside from changes brought upon the surrounding neighborhood by the 1931 opening of the George Washington Bridge, a layout this short was bound to become somewhat outdated over time. Perhaps because of this, the club weathered a variety of economic storms over the years, eventually becoming known as an especially "colorful" place featuring many show business and Mafia personalities.

In the early 1960s, the construction of Interstate 95 literally divided the golf course in two, though some artful rerouting by club professional Alec Ternyei managed to keep an 18-hole sequence of play alive. By the mid-1970s, however, the financial problems became too great, and in 1976 the club closed its doors for the final time.

The 18th green during the 1916 New Jersey Championship, the club's last big event before calling in Donald Ross. (*Golf Illustrated*)

How Engelwood Would Measure Up Today

Like such historic places as Onwentsia and Midlothian, clubs whose long-ago hosting of the U.S. Open serves to illustrate just how dramatically the game has changed.

Lacking room to expand in any meaningful way and already pretty well bunkered, Englewood would essentially have been limited to the precise layout that Donald Ross provided. Not that this was such a bad prospect even in modern terms, but it hardly would have stood out among a plethora of top-quality North Jersey alternatives.

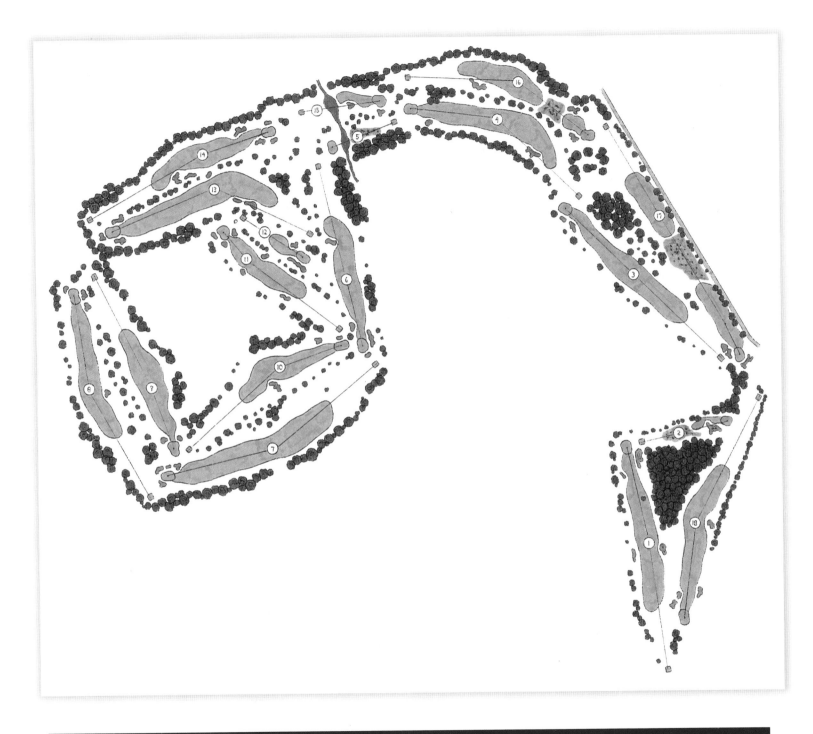

PINEHURST (Number Four)																				
419	162	410	395	141	355	446	408	357	3076	398	305	164	426	390	173	375	514	447	3192	6268
4	3	4	4	3	4	5	4	4	35	4	4	3	4	4	3	4	5	5	36	71

PINEHURST RESORT & COUNTRY CLUB
PINEHURST, NC

Number Four Course, 1912 / 6,268 yards Par-71

There are few names more synonymous with golf course architecture than that of Donald Ross, and no name is more synonymous with Donald Ross than Pinehurst. For there, amid the thickly-forested sandhills of North Carolina, Ross not only designed one of his true masterpieces, the resort's legendary Number Two Course, but also built or rebuilt four more vintage layouts of varying difficulty. And these were no "paper jobs," featuring one site visit and a mailed-in map, either. On the contrary, Pinehurst's were among the most hands-on, finely-tuned golf courses of all time, owing to the architect's constant attention during his amazing 49 years as the resort's winter golf professional.

To backtrack a few steps, Donald Ross was born in Dornoch, Scotland, but spent several years living at St. Andrew's where, like C.B. Macdonald before him and A.W. Tillinghast after, he fell under the influence of Old Tom Morris. Becoming well-versed in Old Tom's principles of sound course architecture, he returned home and served for seven years as Royal Dornoch's Professional before ultimately emigrating to America in 1899.

His first job stateside was as professional and greenskeeper at the Oakley Country Club in Watertown, Massachusetts, where Ross met James Walker Tufts, the developer of Pinehurst. Almost immediately he had found his winter job, a position which required the usual array of teaching and agronomical skills but also allowed time for Ross to establish himself as a fine player (he finished fifth in the 1903 U.S. Open at Baltusrol) and begin his second calling as an architect.

It has been estimated, perhaps generously, that Ross designed as many as 600 courses in his career but if this number is at all accurate, "designed" (as opposed to "built") is certainly the operative word. Indeed, his detractors have even accused Ross of laying out many courses via topographical map without ever setting eyes upon a site, a suggestion which might serve to explain the obvious discrepancies between strategic classics like Seminole and Pinehurst Number Two and many of his lesser-known, less-inspiring projects. Architect Pete Dye seemed to acknowledge these discrepancies when he observed that Ross "designed so many golf courses, but there are probably only twenty of them that ever had that strategy. Those are the ones built by his construction crews."

Because so many foreign hands obviously were involved in a course constructed outside of Ross's supervision, the final product often lacked consistency, making rather laughable such frequently-used phrases as "Ross-style bunkering" and the like. However one constant of the architect's actual, hands-on work was an attention to green positioning and contouring well beyond that of most modern designers. His belief in the importance of smart course management and a strong short game generally yielded a less visually spectacular product filled with gentle, ground-level challenges not always apparent on a course map. Frequently, they required multiple playings to be fully appreciated.

Ross's design work at Pinehurst began in 1901 when, with the 18-hole Number One course already in play, he built the first nine of Number Two. This layout was expanded to 18 by 1907, and by 1910 Number Three would be completed, giving the resort a then-unprecedented 54 holes. So adequate must these facilities have seemed that when Number Four began showing its first signs of life in 1912, it was only as a six-hole practice facility. But amid the constant renovations and expansions affecting the property, it grew to full nine-hole status by 1914 and, eventually, 18 holes in 1919.

In the years immediately to follow, small chunks of yardage were added and subtracted here and there, but the only apparent alteration of real note was the extension of number 18 from a 419-yard par-4 to a 447-yard par-5. The result, by 1925, was a layout measuring 6,268 yards and playing to a par of 71. While very little documentation exists regarding the exact placement of its hazards, several sources have been utilized to create a reasonably good facsimile herein.

Though no rival for the great Number Two, Number Four featured several holes that would still do the property proud today, three of which were the openers. The first, a rather vigorous wake-up call at 419 yards, set the table for the much shorter second, an attractive 162-yarder played across a gaping cross-bunker. The third, another long, straight shot at 410 yards, completed the sequence with a long-iron approach to a green guarded short by two more bunkers.

Following the dogleg-left fourth came the first of two water holes, the attractive 141-yard fifth. With only slight alterations to his routing, Ross could have toughened this one considerably by placing the green flush to the hazard. But it seems that at Pinehurst at least he was reluctant to do so, for even on Number Two he positioned the layout's only water in front of the tee on the par-5 16th where it has seldom if ever affected the better player.

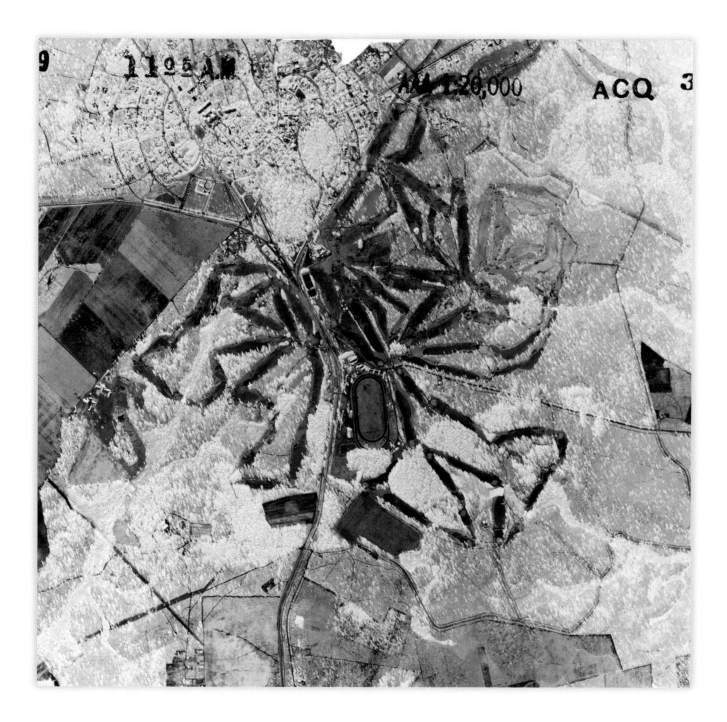

1939 aerial survey of the entire Pinehurst property. The mostly-closed number four course
is upper right, the famous number two at upper center.

Other than the attractive 355-yard sixth, the next really notable hole may have been the 398-yard 10th, a wide two-shotter tempting one to skirt a large fairway bunker nearly 200 yards out in order to open an improved angle of approach.

But it was Number Four's finishers that represented the course's backbone with the long dogleg-left 13th, which required a substantially drawn tee ball, setting the tone.

Strangely, holes 15 and 16 appear actually to have gotten shorter between 1923 and 1925, measuring 203 and 427 yards initially, then 173 and 375 two years later. The former, which came back across the same small pond in play on hole number five, was a bit more formidable at its longer distance while the latter, doglegging sharply right, likely was no bargain either way.

The closers, too, appear to have been made easier along yardage lines, the 17th being shortened from 550 yards to 514, the 18th turned into a fairly simple 447-yard par-5 from an otherwise difficult 419-yard two-shotter.

The reason for such changes? There are no records to say for sure but a reasonable guess might stem from the notion that with Number Two and Number Three already seeing a great deal of tournament activity, a more relaxing, vacation-like atmosphere may have suited old Number Four—or at least have been imposed upon it.

Equally curious is the history of its demise. While many such multicourse clubs experienced economically-driven closings during wartime, Number Four initially lost holes 6 through 14 in 1936, well before America's involvement in World War II and the very same year in which the resort successfully hosted the PGA Championship. The remaining nine holes, not surprisingly, were then abandoned in 1938.

Following the war, and with alterations made by James Walker Tufts's grandson Dick, the layout was reopened in stages. It then remained relatively unchanged until 1973 when Robert Trent Jones remodeled out of existence whatever remained of Ross's work. Subsequent "softening" of the course was done in 1982 but even that version has vanished, being replaced in 1999 by a new Tom Fazio design built upon the same piece of land.

To place Fazio's modern work in comparison with the long-lost Ross design would be unfair. But in a 1978 letter, an aging Dick Tufts rather eloquently commented upon the fate suffered by a layout to which he had obviously given both his time and his heart. He wrote:

"I built this to be an easy pleasant course, but judging by what people say and the very vague plan on the scorecard, I wish the credit could read 'Wrecked by Robert Trent Jones, Golf Course Architect.' Certainly neither Mr. Ross (nor I) would want to be held responsible for anything about the present course."

Amen.

How Pinehurst Would Measure Up Today

As a fine throwback resort course with a handful of very challenging holes. A classic? Not even close. But traditionalists and Ross fans might frequently have chosen it over several distinctly more modern area alternatives.

A great vacation layout.

If we are inclined to believe the oft-cited but dubious estimate of Donald Ross having designed over 600 courses, then we are crowning him, without challenge, the most prolific American golf architect of them all. Naturally, if he built the most courses, there stands a pretty fair chance that he also lost the most—and little evidence exists to suggest otherwise.

But cataloging Ross's other lost courses is no easy task, due not only to space limitation but also to the highly-rural location of much of his work, making its accurate documentation something of a hit-or-miss proposition. Mentioned here then is only a sampling, a group of facilities whose clear documentation makes them the easiest to present in an accurate, representative manner.

Built in 1912, the Country Club of Havana was not only a geographic novelty but also likely the earliest 18-hole Ross design that no longer exists. Located several miles west of the Cuban capital, it was a scenic, palm-laden track routed through a small valley and around the Rio Almendares, creating a number of tricky, character-filled holes. It was also quite difficult, for according to reports published in 1931 the modestly long 6,290-yard layout had hosted players such as Sarazen, Armour, MacDonald Smith, and Johnny Farrell without yielding a single sub-70 score. Curiously, this layout was significantly altered and resequenced during its early years, though precisely when or by whom is unknown.

It is possible that Ross himself did this work when he returned to Cuba in 1927 to build the nearby Havana Biltmore Yacht & Country Club. Located 10 miles west of downtown, this 6,472-yard layout, set upon a bluff above the Gulf of Mexico, was widely considered the island's best course, its par of 70 including a demanding eight 400-plus-yard par-4s. Regrettably, like the Country Club of Havana and the handful of other clubs operating on the island, this bastion of capitalist decadence disappeared soon after Fidel Castro's rise to power in 1959.

The Country Club of Havana, Cuba

Over $150,000 has been spent in creating a magnificent Country Club in the vicinity of the City of Havana.

The eighteen-hole golf course, laid out by Donald Ross, is first-class in every respect. It is not too much to say that few courses anywhere afford greater variety or more interesting features.

Other attractions are tennis courts, a croquet lawn and practice putting greens.

The bay of Mariano nearby affords fine salt water bathing and boating. Ample diversion for both golfers and their families. Splendid roads. Grand views. Delighful climate.

A large and complete Club House with ample accommodations for members, guests and their families.

The club is easily reached by railroad or automobile from Havana, a station being directly on the grounds.

Full provision has been made for visitors who can avail themselves of the privileges of the Club House and course on proper introduction.

Weekly competitions and special tournaments during the winter months.

All rail, via Key West 2½ days.   Direct steamer 3½ days.

ADDRESS P. O. BOX No. 1267, HAVANA, CUBA

1912 advertisement for the Country Club of Havana. (*The American Golfer*)

Just across the Florida Straits lay Ross's Miami Country Club, a course he remodeled and expanded from nine to 18 holes in 1919. Located sightly south of Northwest 20th Street near downtown, it was described in a 1924 *Golf Illustrated* piece as "one of the best ever laid out" by the architect, measuring roughly 6,300 yards and featuring 92 bunkers. A frequent host to winter tournament action, the club was operated briefly as a private facility in the late 1920s before the Depression returned it to the public domain. Long gone from the downtown landscape, its site is today occupied by a section of the Dolphin Expressway, two hospitals and a host of other distinctly nongolf entities.

Moving into Georgia, the Number Two Course at East Lake Country Club (childhood home of Bobby Jones and three-time U.S. Women's Amateur champion Alexa Stirling) was perhaps Ross's highest-profile loss. Located just across Skiff Street from the club's recently restored Number One layout, it was built in 1928 not as a shorter, easier stepchild but as a bona fide 6,725-yard challenge. Less heavily bunkered than Number One, Number Two did include seven par-4s of over 400 yards, likely making it almost as difficult to score upon. In addition, it featured something common to early Southern courses: an alternate set of winter/summer greens, a circumstance made necessary by the relatively primitive agronomic practices of the time. Though Number Two actually came into existence well after both Jones's and Stirling's formative years at the club, its 1960s demise (sold to the government for low-income housing) must fall as a low point in East Lake history.

12th green, Country Club of Havana, circa 1930. (*Golf Illustrated*)

Winter tournament action at Miami Country Club. (R.W. Miller Golf Library)

Up north in New Jersey, where Ross gems like Plainfield, Montclair, and the lesser-known Mountain Ridge carry on his good name, Homestead and an early version of Ridgewood join Englewood as notable losses. Homestead, located in Spring Lake, was a fairly ambitious 1920 design measuring 6,343 yards with a par 72. Ridgewood, on the other hand, was a patch-up job, turning a tight, extremely hilly member-designed course into a layout measuring only 6,045 yards, yet featuring seven par-5s! Not surprisingly, it was abandoned when the club hired A.W. Tillinghast to build their enduringly classic 27-hole facility in 1927.

In New York, the Hudson River Country Club in Yonkers was historically important, beginning life as the Saegkill Country Club, a facility founded in 1895 by the female members of America's oldest enduring club, nearby St. Andrew's. The men took over Saegkill in 1915, however, and refurbished it dramatically, bringing Ross aboard to renovate the golf course fully. His 5,412-yard layout was subsequently altered by William Tucker and lived a quiet, unassuming existence until its doors closed in 1966.

In Philadelphia Ross created the long-departed Sunnybrook Golf Club for a distinguished membership that included talented architect-to-be George Thomas. A 6,430-yard, par-73 layout, Sunnybrook opened in 1915 and featured several fine holes routed across the small

Number Two Course at East Lake. Note alternate winter/summer greens

EAST LAKE																				
473	384	183	426	350	425	381	193	443	3264	408	575	203	434	479	140	374	400	448	3461	6725
5	4	3	4	4	4	4	3	4	35	4	5	3	4	5	3	4	4	4	36	71

creek for which the property was named. Well-heeled enough to survive through the Depression, the club opted to move in 1954 when state highway construction threatened to reconfigure its layout beyond acceptability.

Another defunct Philadelphia-area course was Overbrook where Ross expanded an old nine-holer to 18 in 1920. Upon the completion of his work, this track measured 6,215 yards but played to a demanding par of 70, featuring four two-shotters of at least 420 yards and back-nine par-3s measuring 205 and 233 yards. Though staggered badly by the Depression, Overbrook managed to gut it out for quite some time, ultimately moving to a new site in nearby Radnor in 1952.

Most mysterious among Ross's lost creations was Overhills, a luxury resort-to-be located some 28 miles northeast of Pinehurst in North Carolina. A 1917 article in *Golf Illustrated* trumpeted this as one of the architect's elite layouts, built with an unlimited budget on his choice of 3,500 acres of wooded sandhill country. Strangely, while the writer cited holes 12, 16, 17, and 18 as being of particular merit, the club was listed as having only nine holes in 1927's *American Annual Golf Guide* and by World War II existed strictly as a 3,047-yard, par-35 test. Though likely a fraction of its original self, Overhills remained alive until the early 1990s when the Army bought it for nongolf usage in association with Fort Bragg.

GEORGE C. THOMAS

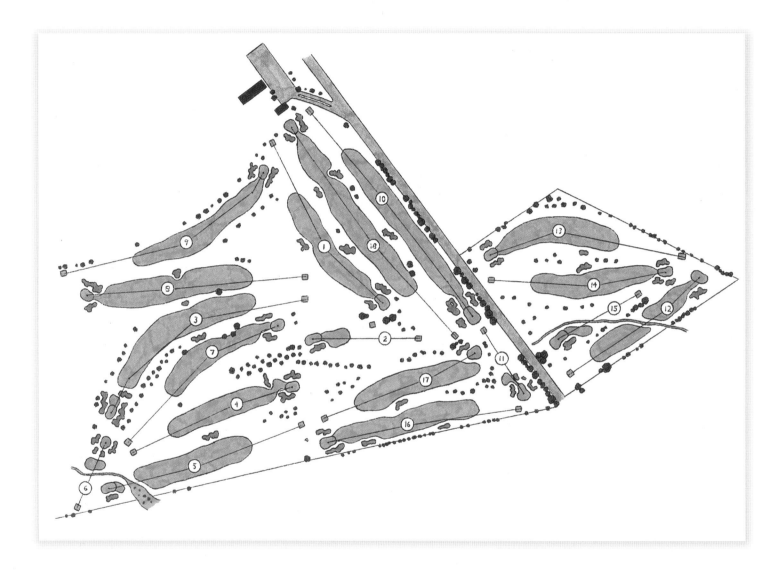

FOX HILLS																				
392	108	484	347	399	135	379	433	469	3146	501	147	315	401	344	191	376	390	516	3181	6327
4	3	5	4	4	3	4	4	5	36	5	3	4	4	4	3	4	4	5	36	72

FOX HILLS GOLF CLUB

CULVER CITY, CA

Opened in 1927 / 6,327 yards Par-72

Among golf's great architects, there can be little doubt that when judging in a worldly, well-rounded context, the most accomplished individual was one George C. Thomas, Jr. Oh, certainly Alister MacKenzie was a medical doctor and military camouflage expert, C.B. Macdonald was a successful stockbroker, and Seth Raynor a professional surveyor and Princeton graduate. But when it came to such categories as maintaining a broad range of interests, doing things to help one's community and that perennial champion, serving one's country, George Thomas was truly a Renaissance man, the runaway, hands-down winner.

Thomas did enjoy the advantage of a strong start in life, being the first-born of an affluent and socially prominent Philadelphia family, but the majority of his accomplishments were achieved in fields far removed from his family's sphere of influence. He was, for example, a genuine military hero, serving as a fighter pilot during World War I and surviving three major crashes. In civilian life he was one of the finest hybridizers of commercial roses in history, creating at least 40 new species, several of which remain popular today. He was also a talented golfer and dog trainer (his English Setter winning Best-of-Breed awards at the 1901 and '03 Westminster shows) and, in later years, an accomplished fisherman and yachtsman. Finally, as a gifted writer, Thomas shared his various areas of expertise in the books *The Practical Book of Outdoor Rose Growing*, *Roses for All American Climates*, *Game Fish of the Pacific* and his classic volume on golf design, *Golf Architecture in America*.

Most accounts of his architectural career rightly focus upon Los Angeles' famous "Thomas Triumvirate," the geographically-close troika of Riviera, Bel Air, and the North Course at Los Angeles Country Club. At the latter, Thomas's classically strategic layout has since been "modernized," resulting in so difficult a test that many longstanding members prefer to play the club's easier South Course. At the gorgeous Bel Air, where a unique canyon-to-canyon routing resulted in one of the most interesting layouts ever crafted, several significant alterations have transformed virtually all of its great holes into duller, more "standardized" versions. At Riviera, however, Thomas's self-proclaimed masterpiece has survived relatively unmolested, a 1939 flood altering three holes but leaving all else pretty much as planned.

Forgotten amid the kudos thrown at the Triumvirate, however, is the fact that Thomas did build several other courses in the Los Angeles area, most of which have today been altered beyond recognition. Granted, these often tended to be somewhat less exciting layouts, making their relative destruction less disappointing than it otherwise might seem. But one additional Thomas design did stand out and might, in generous terms, have even garnered consideration as a fourth L.A. masterpiece were it still with us today: Fox Hills.

Located slightly south of the Triumvirate in Culver City, Fox Hills opened in 1927 as the second of two adjoining courses built by Thomas on rolling, canyon-dotted terrain some four miles inland from the Pacific. Its sister course, originally known as Baldwin Hills Country Club, was soon absorbed by Fox Hills and it was as a single, 36-hole public facility that the club would operate for the duration of its years.

Judging objectively, while Fox Hills' lack of alternate fairways, boomerang greens and the like did leave it a notch beneath Thomas's more interesting top-shelf designs, it blossomed in later years into a long and quite challenging golf course. How difficult? Chosen as site of the 1954 Los Angeles Open, it produced a winning score of three-under-par 281, a total higher than six of the previous seven years when the event had been played at Riviera. It should be noted, though, that by this time the course had grown nearly 350 yards from its original configuration, and it is that shorter (and perhaps somewhat more artistic) version that is presented here.

The layout began innocently enough with a 392-yard par-4 and 108-yard par-3, the latter being extended relatively early on with the addition of an alternate tee measuring 222 yards.

The third, a 484-yard par-5, played down the same shallow canyon as number two before climbing to an elevated green, the open front-right side of which might have allowed a properly-drawn second to run up onto the putting surface.

Though holes four and five ran essentially back and forth, they were quite different in style and difficulty. The former, at 347 yards, was something of a respite while the latter, a fine 399-yarder, required a long, straight tee ball in order to reach a plateau from which an approach across a small dry wash became possible. Later, after being expanded to 449 yards, this would become one of Fox Hills' strongest holes.

Captain Thomas (as he was known after the war) generally created fascinating one-shotters and while those at Fox Hills may not have been among his elite, the sixth, a 135-yarder routed across a valley to a hilltop green, was a real beauty. Though hardly a backbreaker, with its putting surface all but surrounded by bunkers and fronted by a steep grade, it took on dimensions of a "Two or Five" type of proposition.

The remainder of the front side was fairly routine and it wasn't until the player crossed Slauson Avenue to a set of four outlying holes secluded upon the road's north side that things once again picked up in earnest. The first of these, the 315-yard 12th, was fairly narrow and played across a drainage ditch to an elevated, heavily-contoured green. The 401-yard 13th was the foursome's cornerstone, a long dogleg-left which, according to reports, played even longer. The 344-yard 14th then ran uphill to a severely-bunkered green, with the 191-yard 15th coming back down the grade to a long, narrow putting surface pinched by sand and the drainage ditch.

Slipping back across the road, one faced three solid finishers beginning with the 376-yard par-4 16th. Eventually listed as long as 480 yards, this hole always remained at least somewhat manageable in that it was one of the few truly flat ones in sight. Additionally its left greenside bunker favored a drive aimed to the right, safely away from the left-side boundary fence.

Following the 390-yard 17th, its second shot played downhill to a green set gently into a hillside, Fox Hills finished with a final birdie opportunity at the 516-yard 18th, another rolling-fairway sort with a gradual upgrade leading into the green.

Once extended to its 1954 length of 6,972 yards, Fox Hills remained one of Southern California's toughest and most popular public layouts for many years. Ultimately, however, the value of its appreciating Culver City real estate simply became too great, leading to a sell off and the construction of both the Fox Hills Mall and the countless other businesses and residences currently occupying the former 36-hole site.

How Fox Hills Would Measure Up Today

In its 6,900-plus-yard modern configuration, Fox Hills would definitely remain one of the country's tougher (and better) public facilities, likely usurping the city's fine Rancho Park as the occasional Los Angeles Open or Senior Tour site. Unfortunately, one senses that this longer version may have lost a good deal of the charm possessed by Thomas's more intimate original—a sad but seemingly inevitable by-product of keeping up with the times.

On paper at least, all but two of George Thomas's classic designs still exist—sort of.

Third green, Baldwin Hills GC, 400 yards, par-4. (Painting by Mike Miller)

After Fox Hills, the second departee was its sister course, the former Baldwin Hills Golf Club. Measuring 6,440 yards with a par of 72, Baldwin Hills featured the same hilly terrain as its neighbor, as well as some wonderfully artistic Thomas & Bell bunkering, though its three sub 500-yard par fives and several short two-shotters probably made it a bit easier to score upon. Becoming Fox Hills Golf Club's West Course soon after its birth, this layout remained a Southern California favorite until its development-induced demise.

One other excellent Thomas work, La Cumbre Country Club in Santa Barbara, still exists, but hardly in a form that The Captain would recognize. Rebuilt by Thomas and Billy Bell in 1925, La Cumbre was genuinely something special, featuring several excellent lakefront holes on its front nine as well as the 416-yard canyon-crossing sixteenth, one of the most spectacular par fours ever built. Like many courses in California, a World War II-era closing dramatically affected the La Cumbre layout, setting the table for the series of modern "renovations" which have all but ruined it. The legendary 16th, it should be noted, still remains—but in so altered a state that one of golf's most knowledgeable current architects could not even locate it upon his first visit.

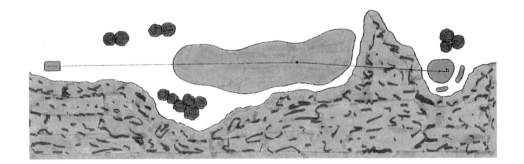

The classic 16th at La Cumbre, today altered beyond recognition.

A.W. Tillinghast

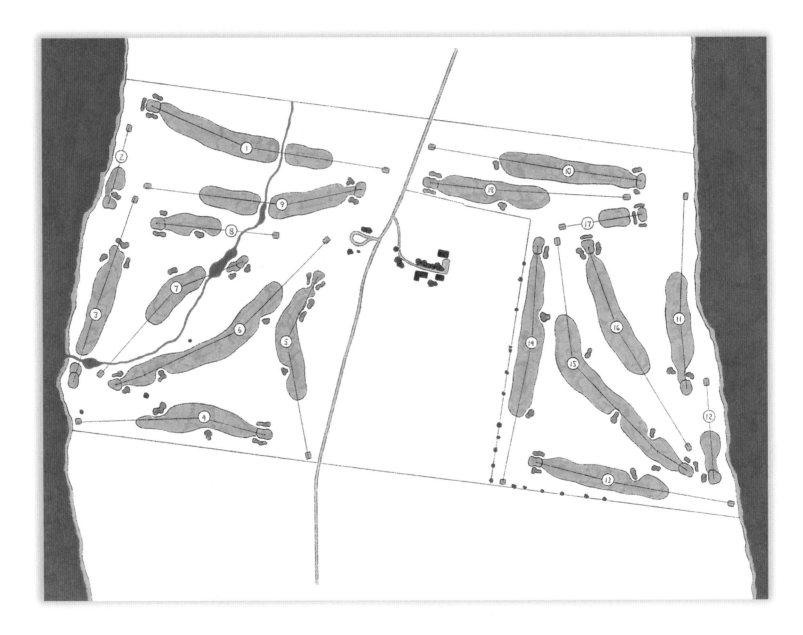

BEAVER TAIL																			
478	137	366	385	342	515	350	225	435	3233	408	354	175	370	426	538	400	152	367	3190	6423
5	3	4	4	4	5	4	3	4	36	4	4	3	4	4	5	4	3	4	35	71

BEAVER TAIL GOLF CLUB

JAMESTOWN, RI

Opened in 1925 / 6,423 yards Par-71

Though golf course design, like fine art, can only be judged in a subjective manner, it is safe to say that any list of its all-time great practitioners must include the self-billed "Dean of American-born architects," Mr. Albert Warren Tillinghast.

The son of well-to-do parents, Tillie grew up in the affluent Philadelphia suburb of Frankford but followed few of the educational or professional conventions of his class. Misspending his youth in all manner of social and antisocial ways, he managed to run with a street gang, drop out of several schools and, apparently, skip college altogether, all by the tender age of 20. Thankfully, prior to advancing too far down a one-way street to incorrigibility, the young Tillinghast discovered the game of golf which, in effect, saved him.

Ultimately becoming a fine amateur player (he finished 25th in the 1910 U.S. Open and competed favorably in several U.S. Amateurs), he took advantage of his economic freedom by making an 1896 excursion to the British Isles. There, at St. Andrew's, he became friendly with that most legendary of golf icons, Old Tom Morris, a relationship which greatly enhanced the young Philadelphian's appreciation for the game's history and traditions.

It was not until 1909 that the then thirty-four-year-old Tillie began dabbling in architecture, and then only because family friend Charles Worthington was building a resort in Shawnee-on-Delaware, Pennsylvania, and decided that he needed a golf course. When this layout (still very much in business at the present-day Shawnee Inn) proved to be both well thought-of and a surprisingly enjoyable endeavor, Tillinghast's attentions promptly turned to course design full-time.

By 1915 his reputation had so expanded that he made trips to Florida, Texas, and California, where the St. Petersburg Country Club, Atlantic Beach Country Club, Brackenridge Park, and San Francisco Golf Club all opened during that year. By the early 1920s, with high-profile 36-hole masterpieces like Baltusrol and Winged Foot under his belt, he had, without question, "made it."

Naturally then, Tillinghast was an obvious candidate when, in 1925, a wealthy Rhode Islander named Audley H. Clarke thought it time to build himself a golf course.

But Mr. Clarke's facility was not to be just another rich man's playground. To begin with, it would be located upon his family's ancestral Jamestown farmland, a concept made special by the property's marvelous location at the southern tip of Conanicut Island, on bluffs overlooking the waters of Narragansett Bay, Rhode Island Sound, and the Atlantic Ocean. It would also be noteworthy in a more novel way, for while some reports have classified Beaver Tail as Audley Clarke's private estate course, local newspaper articles of the period indicated something quite different.

In July of 1925, the *Providence Journal* reported that the golf course would "be open to all summer cottagers and summer hotel guests coming to the island upon payment of ordinary golf club fees." Further, it was Clarke's ultimate plan to bequeath both the farm and golf course to the town upon his death with the hope that its drawing power might lead to more people settling in the area. "I have but one desire," he went on to tell the *Journal,* "and that is to see Jamestown properly placed on the map." [As an aside, it should be mentioned that Clarke also requested—and received—a 50% reduction in his property taxes in association with building Beaver Tail, but since he promptly donated $2,500 of that money toward the purchase of a new town fire truck, we must accept his motives more or less at face value.]

Tillinghast, for his part, was apparently excited by the project as well. Having already completed a remodeling of the nearby Newport Country Club in 1924, he was brought aboard at Beaver Tail by Findlay Douglas, noted golfer, friend of Audley Clarke, and all-around project consultant. Upon his first visit to the property, Tillie commented, "Nature laid out this course. Man can do nothing to improve upon its work." Sounds like the P.R. dialogue recited, nearly verbatim, by so many salesmen/designers today? Perhaps, but Tillinghast apparently genuinely believed it, initially planning not a single man-made bunker throughout the 18 holes.

Though sand hazards would eventually figure into the completed layout, Beaver Tail was one of America's most natural courses, playing through open meadows and along ocean-front bluffs, its landscape dotted with only the occasional tree, its every hole affected by the ever-present sea breezes.

It began nondescriptly with a 478-yard par-5 devoid of major danger. But just that quickly the player had reached land's end, with holes two and three running southward along the southern tip of Narragansett Bay, their tees perched 40 to 70 feet above the adjacent beach. The second, a 137-yard one-shotter, played to a small green flanked left by sand and right by the bluffs. The third, a drive and mid-iron at 366 yards, required a tee ball avoiding three fairway bunkers, then a steady approach to a bluffside green also guarded in front by a brook.

Following two more mid-length par-4s, the front nine closed with a run of four of Beaver Tail's best holes.

The 515-yard sixth was called Brook, so named for the meandering hazard which flanked the final third of its right side.

The 350-yard seventh was known as Pond, its green being situated adjacent to the point where the brook widened. Here only a drive and short iron were required, the former threaded between brook and fairway bunker, the latter played to one of the course's tighter green sites.

After the obvious challenge of the 225-yard eighth, one turned for home at the 435-yard ninth, a straightaway par-4 with one notable obstacle: another small pond crossing the fairway, causing many a longer player to lay up off the tee.

Its routing almost a mirror image of the outer half, Beaver Tail's back nine began with a solid par-4 at the 408-yard 10th, an opener which again served to take us back to water's edge. This time the beachfront 11th and 12th bordered the northern reaches of Rhode Island Sound but were otherwise similar to their corresponding holes on the outward half, particularly the 175-yard 12th where a single bunker guarded the green's inland side.

The 370-yard 13th hugged close to the property line as did the longer 14th, whose left-side out-of-bounds came in the form of the Clarke homesite. The 15th and 16th then did a long out-and-back, setting the stage for a pair of finishers whose "as built" configurations differed significantly from the architect's original blueprints.

Named "Tilly's Rest" (obviously not by Tillie himself who likely would have spelled his own nickname properly), the 152-yard 17th was Beaver Tail's second shortest hole and played to a tight, highly-symmetrical green complex. On paper, however, it was drawn with a larger green angling left-to-right behind a pair of much larger cross-bunkers. No reason for the variance is recorded.

The par-4 18th, rather inexplicably named Dublin Road, differed primarily in terms of yardage. On Tillie's blueprint it measured 418 yards, in reality only 367. Yet the hole still closed things out in challenging fashion as its narrow green was threatened both by sand and the boundary of the Clarke homestead tight along its leftward flank.

Though Audley Clarke fulfilled the first part of his plan by successfully building so fine a golf course, the latter part—donating the facility to the town upon his death—never panned out. Hard times brought on by the Depression affected the course's viability dramatically and it was last used by United States Naval officers stationed in the area during World War II. Following the war, the layout was abandoned with half of the land eventually being sold off for subdivision. A mid-1990s plan to rebuild nine original holes and add nine new ones ultimately fell through, leaving Beaver Tail, at least for the moment, as but another Golden Age golfing memory.

How Beaver Tail Would Measure Up Today

As the sort of track that would be a cult classic—except that its spectacular seaside location likely would draw too much attention to remain cultish. With a bit of obligatory lengthening, it would have been a typically strong and varied Tillinghast layout, its routing making wind a constant factor in the grandest British tradition. Not on par with Tillie's marquee designs perhaps, but a substantial and gorgeous test—and something of a standout in a New England region surprisingly devoid of topflight classics.

FRESH MEADOW																				
437	395	391	188	578	428	412	435	143	3407	385	413	155	448	219	424	587	373	404	3408	6815
4	4	4	3	5	4	4	4	3	35	4	4	3	4	3	4	5	4	4	35	70

FRESH MEADOW COUNTRY CLUB
FLUSHING, NY

Opened in 1922 / 6,815 yards Par-70

From the moment of its inception, the Fresh Meadow Country Club traveled in style. The brainchild of an affluent community leader named Nathan Jonas, it endeavored to have only the finest of recreational facilities, not the least of which would be a golf course capable of challenging the world's finest competitors in Major championship play. Mr. Jonas also robbed the treasury to hire Gene Sarazen as his golf professional in 1925 and twice built state-of-the-art clubhouses, the initial version burning down just nine days after the club's opening.

With the bar raised so high, it is hardly surprising that Jonas chose A.W. Tillinghast as his golf course architect, nor that Tillie responded with one of his most notorious layouts. A Winged Foot-style track, Fresh Meadow stretched beyond 6,800 yards from the championship tees while playing to a demanding par of 70. Tough? Without question, though Tillie himself considered it a bit less so than Winged Foot, owing to its slightly more forgiving greenside bunkering. Great? In many ways yes, for while this was hardly the architect's most varied design, it did carry many of the traits so highly thought of on his other high-profile championship courses. Additionally, no less than five of the club's holes were selected in the aforementioned 1934 *The American Golfer* series identifying the country's finest, a particularly strong recommendation.

In any case, it didn't take long for Fresh Meadow to make its mark, being selected to host first the 1930 PGA Championship, then the 1932 U.S. Open. Sarazen, still serving as club pro, was defeated in the final of the then-match play PGA when Tommy Armour holed a 15-foot putt on the 36th hole to beat him. Convinced that he'd been affected by something he called the

"Home Pro Jinx," the sometimes irascible Sarazen took a job at the nearby Lakeville Club the following summer in preparation for 1932—and damned if he didn't return to Fresh Meadow and win that U.S. Open.

Sarazen's final round of 66, called by Grantland Rice "the most remarkable finish any golf open ever knew," became a benchmark in the history of U.S. Open scoring, as did the fact that The Squire played the final 27 holes in an even 100 strokes, a feat to which much subsequent literary tribute was paid. But this record finish still only added up to a six-over-par winning total and with players like Armour, Paul Runyan, Jug McSpaden, Craig Wood and MacDonald Smith all failing to break 300, a good argument can be made that the golf course did in fact stand up.

Eventual champion Tommy Armour putting at the ninth green during the final match of the 1930 PGA Championship, with Gene Sarazen looking on. The eighth green, with its enormous right-side bunker, is visible beyond. (*The American Golfer*)

Tillinghast favored starting the golfer with a long, challenging par-4 and at Fresh Meadow it was a 437-yarder with a fairway guarded by five bunkers. Thankfully, the relatively small green allowed ample room for a run-up shot, a trait common to most of Fresh Meadow's putting surfaces, though generally through a bit narrower opening.

If anywhere on the layout there was a genuine respite, it was at the 395- and 391-yard second and third. Here were two medium-length par-4s that obviously presented birdie opportunities, though their odd routing, curling around a large incursion into an otherwise symmetrical property line, brought out-of-bounds very much into play. This was especially true at the third where the early turn of the dogleg virtually mandated that the better player fly his drive over the O.B., the challenge being the estimation of just how far.

Following the 188-yard fourth came an especially difficult stretch beginning with the 578-yard fifth, a hole cited by two-time Masters champion Horton Smith as one of the finest he had ever played. Smith also selected the 428-yard sixth among his favorite par-4s and it was, without question, a real Tillinghast beauty. Though obviously fairly long for its day,

Approach to the 18th green, 1932. (*Golf Illustrated*)

number six was also highly strategic, requiring one to skirt the edge of a small pond which guarded the right side of the driving area if the ideal line of approach were to be had. A most difficult test, it may well have been Sarazen's birdie here (off a splendid two-iron hit to four feet) that jump-started his Sunday run to victory.

The 412-yard seventh and 435-yard eighth continued a stretch of back-and-forth routing but did so demandingly, the former requiring a drawn tee ball to avoid tall trees on the left and a single bunker right, the latter played to a green guarded by one of Tillinghast's largest-ever bunkers.

The outward half closed with the short 143-yard ninth, little more than an eight or nine iron played to one of the course's most severe green complexes. As an interesting footnote, Sarazen scored another important final-round birdie here when he chose to abandon the conservative "no three putts" approach he'd used for the first 62 holes, aggressively striking a downhill 15-footer despite the dangerous back-to-front slope of the green. Why the change of tactics from so tricky a spot? Because during his years working for the club, his pro shop was located only yards away, providing innumerable hours of practice putting upon the ninth green's otherwise-scary contours.

Did he say "*Home Pro Jinx?*"

The back nine began with a fine mid-length par-4 of 385 yards, a dogleg-left to a well-bunkered green placed perilously close to the club's entrance road (out-of-bounds). The 413-yard 11th and 155-yard 12th were similarly attractive, both offering handsome doses of the famous Tillinghast aesthetic polish. At the 11th a punchbowl-like green welcomed slightly wayward approaches, making it one of the club's more forgiving holes. But number 12 was just the opposite, its narrow, elevated putting surface tending to repel poorly-struck balls into one of five surrounding bunkers.

Things returned to their standard imposing proportion at the 448-yard 13th, then again at the rather interesting 219-yard 14th. Clearly not a replica of any previously-built par-3, the latter's primary features were two enormous cross-bunkers (really only slightly in play) and a small green laid perilously close to both woods and a significant fallaway immediately to its left.

Gene Sarazan blasts to the final green, 1932 U.S. Open. This up-and-down gave him 66 and his second Open championship.
(*Golf Illustrated*)

The 15th, dead-straight and 424 yards long, may have ranked higher among Tillinghast's stiffest creations than any hole on the back nine, due primarily to the steepness and depth of the greenside bunkers.

Then, following a very long par-5, one faced a most interesting drive at the 373-yard 17th where a wide fairway swung left-to-right, snuggling close to a left-side stone wall marking out-of-bounds. Due to the relatively early turn of the dogleg, the better player was virtually compelled to skirt its corner, for laying back would mean an overly long approach to this small, tightly-bunkered green.

The 18th, measuring 404 yards, was not an especially thought-provoking finisher but it did require a long, accurate tee shot. Anything less might bring into play three crossbunkers some 50 yards shy of the green, and otherwise render the very narrow putting surface an especially difficult target.

Despite its affluence and the national prominence associated with its two Major championships, Fresh Meadow eventually felt the same pressures of suburban expansion that befell so many of its Queens brethren. As was the case with its close neighbor Pomonok, postwar development simply came too hard and too fast, and in 1946 the club was sold to developers. Interestingly, the membership didn't dissolve but instead bought out the same Lakeville Club to which Gene Sarazen had moved some 15 years earlier, taking over its C.H. Alison design and renaming it Fresh Meadow, the moniker under which it continues doing business to this day.

How Fresh Meadow Would Measure Up Today

Though hardly Tillinghast's most artistic design, Fresh Meadow seems the sort that would have aged well, riding who knows how many more Major events into the pantheon of high-profile American championship facilities. Indeed its spacious property would in many ways have constituted the ideal modern tournament site with ample room to lengthen the course to well over 7,000 yards and, most importantly, to house dozens of highly-priced corporate tents.

Priorities!

NORWOOD																				
420	404	137	375	388	475	167	390	384	3140	455	304	210	518	380	186	475	374	420	3322	6462
4	4	3	4	4	5	3	4	4	35	5	4	3	5	4	3	5	4	4	37	72

NORWOOD COUNTRY CLUB
WEST LONG BRANCH, NJ

Year opened (unknown) / 6,462 yards Par-72

Though he was born and raised in suburban Philadelphia and died in Toledo, Ohio, A.W. Tillinghast's memory is surely most associated with his many years spent in the New York metropolitan area. During these halcyon days, which essentially extended throughout the 1920s, Tillie owned an expensive columned home in the upscale suburb of Harrington Park, New Jersey, commuting each day to his office at 33 West 42nd Street in Manhattan. Ever a man of taste and style, he relied neither upon mass transit nor driving himself, instead arriving each morning in a chauffeur-driven vehicle, adding yet another flourish to the already-considerable Tillinghast mystique.

The combination of such flamboyance with genuinely exceptional talent ought naturally to add up to something and in Tillie's case, it was a near-dominance of the New York area's golf design business. To what degree did he control this market? Between 1920 and 1935, he was responsible for the design or redesign of a remarkable 40 Metropolitan area courses! George Thomas's monopoly of Los Angeles? Donald Ross's fiefdom in Pinehurst? No contest. In ever-fertile Westchester County alone, Tillie worked on 14 separate layouts, nearly all of which remain in play today.

Of course, not all of his creations were on the Major-Championship scale of Winged Foot, Baltusrol, or Fresh Meadow, and it is not at all surprising that, stacked up against such heavyweight neighbors, some fine layouts such as Fenway, Wykagyl, or Metropolis have tended to slip by unnoticed. And to this list of excellent but out-of-the-limelight courses, one could well add the Norwood Country Club of West Long Branch, New Jersey—were it still alive today.

Golf in the Long Branch area dates back to before the turn of the century, and a course did exist on the Norwood site prior to Tillinghast's arrival. But Tillie's work transformed the property completely, replacing a rudimentary facility with a layout which, save for a slight lack of length, mirrored many of his best for style and challenge.

It began in the architect's favored fashion, with a pair of strapping par-4s measuring 420 and 404 yards. The former was fairly straightforward in manner, doglegging slightly left to a small, well-guarded green. The second was a tad more thought-provoking, bearing some resemblance to the shorter 17th at Fresh Meadow in that it angled left-to-right past a left-side out-of-bounds fence. The fairway grew gradually narrower as one went along, its more dangerous left side opening the best second-shot angle.

The Norwood clubhouse, 1922—today the local community center. (*Golf Illustrated*)

At 137 yards, the third (known as Dainty Drop) was an eye-catcher, and somewhat unique to the Tillinghast portfolio. Not that there was anything particularly different about his building a small, tightly-bunkered green, but the bunkering on this short one-shotter was especially inspired, its free-form shaping extending well back into the fairway in a sort of Charles Alison meets Dr. MacKenzie hybrid.

Following a pair of mid-length par-4s requiring more accuracy than muscle, the player reached the 475-yard sixth, a short and very reachable par-5. Tillinghast generally did not think much of three-shotters, often suggesting that there were very few good golf holes measuring in excess of 500 yards (though he himself seemed to build a good many of them). In the case of number six, its diminutive size certainly made things interesting, inviting most anyone capable of striking the ball solidly to have a go at the green with his second. A set of cross-bunkers threatened a poorly struck shot, however, and a particularly large trap ringed the back half of the putting surface.

Tillie was, on the other hand, a powerful believer in the importance of excellent par-3s and Norwood's seventh, all 167 yards of it, did little to tarnish that view. Its bunkers reflecting more of the rough-edged wildness of MacKenzie than the sculpting of Tillinghast, number seven required a mid-iron approach played to an extremely narrow putting surface, the gentle curvature of which offered several challenging pin placements.

If a single factor tends to separate a course like Norwood from the Baltusrols and Winged Foots, it is the length of its par-4s. The higher-profile layouts—often periodically lengthened in preparation for modern championships—feature numerous two-shotters stretching well beyond 400 yards while the Norwoods of the world tend to offer holes of similar style and character but a bit less brawn. The eighth and ninth (at 390 and 384 yards) were fine examples of this, and were in turn followed by another reachable par-5, the 455-yard 10th.

Following the deceptively difficult drive-and-pitch 11th (appropriately named Duffer's Delusion), the 210-yard 12th played back across an enormous short-right bunker. Requiring a long-iron or wooden approach, this was definitely one of Norwood's most difficult holes, particularly if the fronting sand intimidated one leftward, toward nearby out-of-bounds.

Among the club's closers, the 15th and 18th stood out as being especially noteworthy. The former, a 186-yard par-3, played across a large expanse of sandy waste to a narrow green pinched between bunkers. The latter, a 420-yarder, was a fine example of Tillie's preference for long, difficult par-4 finishers. Returning the player to the clubhouse for the first time, it did suffer the modest annoyance of running directly into the setting sun, a circumstance which only amplified the already-steep challenge of a long-iron second played into a severely bunkered green.

Though comparable to many of the Metropolitan area's famous layouts, Norwood never developed a large reputation during its roughly 30-year existence. Located close to the Atlantic shoreline and within relatively easy commuting distance of New York City, its land inevitably drew the attention of developers and was ultimately sold off and subdivided in the early 1950s.

How Norwood Would Measure Up Today

A notch or two beneath the New York/New Jersey elite, but its wild bunkering and large doses of Tillinghast polish would still guarantee it a spot on any list of noteworthy area courses.

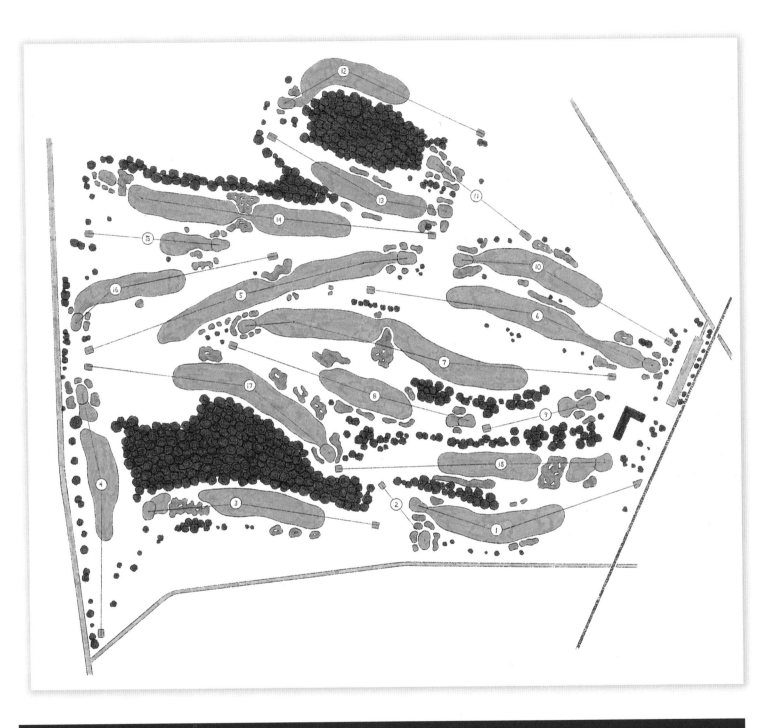

ST ALBANS																				
353	118	343	362	502	445	555	407	154	3239	353	177	326	303	517	212	321	425	402	3036	6275
4	3	4	4	5	4	5	4	3	36	4	3	4	4	5	3	4	4	4	35	71

ST. ALBANS COUNTRY CLUB
ST. ALBANS, NY

Remodeled in 1923 / 6,275 yards Par-71

Though every golf architect prefers a virgin piece of land to develop from the ground up, it is a fact of professional life that there is much money to be made redesigning layouts previously built by others. In the early years, such wholesale rebuilds were sparked by important equipment advances with shorter turn-of-the-century layouts quickly becoming obsolete in the face of livelier golf balls and steel shafts. Later, under the postwar influence of Robert Trent Jones, older courses were steamrolled in attempts at creating "championship" layouts. These 7,000-yard monstrosities had one primary mission: to stand up to modern professionals who, unless the club served as an annual PGA Tour venue, would never play a single competitive round there in the first place. Finally today, in a happy twist of irony, a healthy living can be made by architects specializing in restoration—that is, recreating for older clubs the very same original features so avidly demolished by their green committees some 30-40 years earlier.

Economic reality being what it is, virtually all of the most famous architects of the Golden Age took on regular reconstructive work, though few people seem aware of to how great a degree. For example, more than half of the layouts generally credited to the great A.W. Tillinghast were actually redesigns, some quite thorough, others representing the alteration of just a handful of holes. Further, three of his most famous projects, Quaker Ridge and the Upper and Lower courses at Baltusrol, were themselves alterations of smaller, more limited originals.

Another such overhaul took place at the St. Albans Golf Club in St. Albans, New York, a pleasant, semisuburban neighborhood located slightly north of today's John F. Kennedy Airport in southern Queens. Dating back to 1915, the St. Albans club was one of the New York area's finest, its membership made up of affluent conservative politicians, lawyers, and bankers who clearly valued their privacy. That Babe Ruth considered the course to be his favorite, it has been reported, came as distinctly unwelcomed news to such a flock. For much like the Timber Point members who preferred mosquitoes to the tourists who might frequent the area without them, St. Albans was comprised of the sort of people who would happily pass on the Bambino's praise if such would keep their organization out of the limelight.

The club originally commissioned the Scottish professional Willie Park, Jr. to build their golf course in 1915. Little beyond scorecards exists to document the specifics of that layout but a comparison with yardages listed following Tillinghast's 1923 appearance suggests that a fair degree of Park's original configuration remained intact, albeit resequenced. It is unlikely, however, that much of the prolific bunkering that flavored the course during its pre-World War II heyday was created by the Scotsman, and it was this impressive usage of sand that gave St. Albans so much of its character.

The 1930 Metropolitan Amateur. Maurice McCarthy, Jr. wins his second straight. (*Golf Illustrated*)

The post-1923 Tillinghast layout started with a gentle 353-yard dogleg right followed by the tiny 118-yard second, little more than a pitch but one requiring real accuracy to find a tightly guarded putting surface.

The first of Tillie's really grand bunkering came at the 343-yard third, a tree-lined hole requiring an approach played across a huge, free-formed hazard stretching nearly 75 yards in length. Then, following another mid-length two-shotter at the fourth, the terrain opened up a bit and the challenge began in earnest.

The fifth ran northward, its 502 yards likely reachable in two but made dangerous by a total of 15 bunkers positioned en route. Realistically, several of these hazards were likely intended more to steer players away from neighboring tees and greens than as primary obstacles, but the hole was a solid one nonetheless.

The 445-yard sixth was St. Albans' longest par-4, its second shot slipping between a pair of large cross-bunkers to a green positioned adjacent to the clubhouse. This was followed in turn by the club's longest hole of any sort, the 555-yard seventh, the first of its two par-5s to hint at a famous design concept which Tillie claimed as his own, the Hell's Half Acre.

The 407-yard eighth was another demanding test, its wide fairway flanked by significant bunkering, then narrowing markedly as it approached a small, heavily wooded green. The well-bunkered ninth, only a short- to mid-iron at 154 yards, then completed the outward half.

The back nine began similarly to the front with a 353-yard par-4 followed again by a one-shotter, in this case the 177-yard 11th. This relatively diminutive stretch continued at the short par-4 12th and 13th, measuring 326 and 303 yards respectively. These two-shotters were hardly pushovers, however, playing across wooded terrain with the latter being especially well-bunkered.

The 517-yard 14th was the second Hell's Half Acre-like hole, though in this case, with sand crossing the fairway at about the 300-yard mark, the hazard might reasonably have affected the long hitter's drive more than any competent player's second.

Like many Tillinghast designs, St. Albans closed with a pair of fine par-4s beginning with the 425-yard 17th, a long dogleg-right routed along the edge of heavy woods. Its fairway bunkered profusely down the left side (though again mostly in locations protective of the neighboring eighth hole), this number six handicap hole required a long and accurate approach to a green three-quarters ringed by both sand and forest.

The 402-yard 18th was perhaps the club's most difficult driving test, featuring a long bunker on the right and another larger hazard replacing the fairway just past the 300-yard mark. With one's tee shot properly placed, however, this otherwise-demanding closer became reasonably manageable.

On the whole, Tillinghast's St. Albans track, though built more along the lines of Norwood than Winged Foot or Baltusrol, was a varied, challenging, and aesthetically neat layout despite its modest size. Evidence suggests that it did edge past 6,300 yards by the early 1930s but it was never significantly expanded, a curious point considering the amount of buffering land available and the fact that Willie Park's original had at one time measured 6,438 yards.

Though it did host the 1930 Metropolitan Amateur (won by Maurice McCarthy, Jr.), St. Albans truly did shun the limelight, making its eventual demise little better documented than its quiet, unassuming existence. Like The Lido and several other area courses, it was taken over by the Navy during World War II, an occupancy from which the financially troubled club never truly recovered. Following the war it would serve as the site of a Navy hospital for some 30 years while also having some of its land deeded to New York State. Today a Veterans Administration Extended Care Center sits upon the property, leaving yet another of Queens' topflight courses as a long-buried museum piece.

How St. Albans Would Measure Up Today

Though far from backbreaking, St. Albans would be another of those second-tier Tillinghast gems that dot so much of the Metropolitan area landscape. Like the departed Norwood and many others still with us, it would be revered for its lineage, and play as a fun and interesting test. Perhaps still a potential Met Amateur site and maybe even a star baseball player's favorite—but not quite the layout of regional note that it was in its heyday.

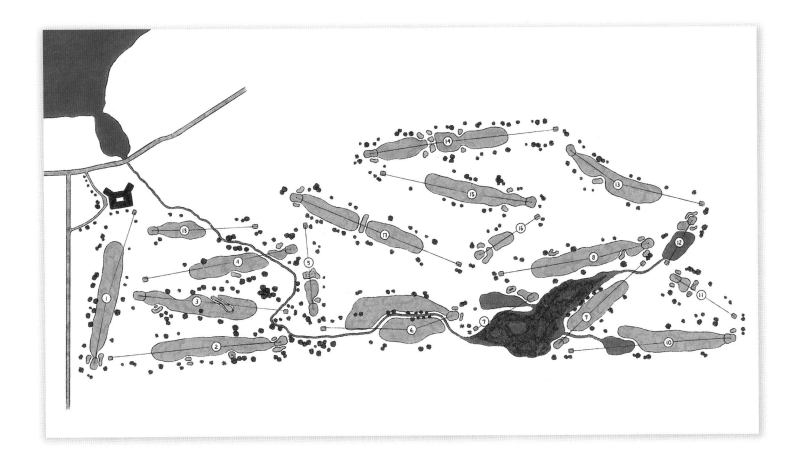

ST PETERSBURG																				
410	435	370	385	210	350	158	390	318	3026	410	197	110	430	518	428	172	459	330	3054	6080
4	4	4	4	3	4	3	4	4	34	4	3	3	4	5	4	3	5	4	35	69

ST. PETERSBURG COUNTRY CLUB
ST. PETERSBURG, FL

Opened in 1915 / 6,080 yards Par-69

Though Florida's Gold Coast has remained a premier winter locale since its initial development at the top of the twentieth century, far less attention has traditionally been paid to the state's "other" coast on the beautiful Gulf of Mexico. Yet even in the late nineteenth century, as Henry Flagler's railway was marching steadily southward toward Miami and Key West, Henry Plant's budding Atlantic Coast Line Railroad was bringing economic viability to the Gulf side, placing such previously sleepy towns as Tampa and St. Petersburg more prominently upon the map.

Development here followed much the same pattern as across the state, making land sales and resort building among the uppermost of priorities. Naturally the need for golf courses to supplement both of these pursuits was apparent so, once again, outside help was called in. It was probably transplanted Scotsman John Duncan Dunn, in his capacity as Director of Golf Planning for Plant's company, who made the first significant architectural impact in the area, though his brother Seymour and that earliest of design vagabonds, Tom Bendelow, had their hands in the pot as well. As was also the case on the East Coast, none of the Golden Age's most famous architects entered the region until a bit later on, with the first such recorded work belonging to A.W. Tillinghast at St. Petersburg Country Club in 1915.

The club—located at the intersection of Park Street and Seventh Avenue North, immediately adjacent to Boca Ciega Bay—was a major civic undertaking at the time, and just what possessed the founders to hire a faraway architect with only one original course thus far to his credit remains a mystery. Yet such perhaps were the persuasive powers of Tillinghast, who also landed projects in such far-flung locales as Jacksonville, San Francisco, and San Antonio during that same year. And while the layout that he built in St. Petersburg will hardly go down as a masterpiece, its initial configuration does provide a fascinating glimpse of an eccentric, self-taught designer still very much in his formative stages.

1926 Jungle Club advertisement. One can almost hear the "famous Gangplank Orchestra." (*Golf Illustrated*)

Measuring a relatively paltry 6,080 yards, this initial version blended a curious mix of both the rudimentary (geometric bunkering, numerous hazardless greens) and the creative, showcasing Tillinghast's innate talents within the rather constrictive framework of the prevalent design styles of the day. Later the course would have some of its green complexes altered, likely by club professional Ernest Anderson during the summer of 1925. Published reports at this time also indicated a lengthening of several holes, but the 1931 edition of *The American Annual Golf Guide* still listed the course at 6,079 yards and a comparison of World War II-era aerial surveys with an early course map suggest that little if any expansion actually took place. And a further testimonial to Tillie's work: with the exception of moving the 18th green, his original routing was retained throughout the club's existence, its fine use of four ponds and a single, wandering brook apparently satisfying several sets of owners and their varied development plans.

The most eventful of these plans took place, not surprisingly, during the Roaring Twenties when, in 1925, the original clubhouse was replaced with a formal garden, a small boat basin filled in, and a luxurious resort hotel known as The Jungle Club built. This widely advertised hostelry apparently enjoyed a fair run of success, though the golf course (which eventually became a real estate subdivision) would survive long after the hotel fell out of fashion. It should also be noted that the layout presented here is circa 1942, and we will likely never know precisely which greenside bunkers were original and which were added by Ernest Anderson (or others) in the interim.

Green of the short par-4 ninth, circa 1925, the water hazard just out of view to the right. (*American Golfer*)

Tillinghast's touch was immediately visible on opening par-4s of 410 and 435 yards, both played to well-bunkered green complexes, the latter of which was also threatened somewhat by the creek. This hazard again popped up in front of the green at the 385-yard fourth, a nice mid-length par-4 requiring careful placement of both drive and approach.

The creek was even more in play at the sixth, a 350-yarder whose green was perched just above its meandering reach. Notably, the left-side fairway, from which one's approach did not require any sort of forced carry, was not a Tillinghast original, apparently being added in the years preceding World War II.

As the creek emptied into Willow Pond, so came the 158-yard seventh, crossing the water diagonally with its all-or-nothing mid-iron. The drive-and-pitch ninth later doubled back to

Late 1920s aerial photo suggests both the grandeur of the Jungle Club and
the flatness of the Florida terrain. (St. Petersburg Museum of History)

the pond's northern banks, its tiny green potentially driveable but likely taking kindly to a more conservative approach.

Following back-to-back par-3s at holes 11 and 12 (the latter played to a tiny, punchbowl-style green), the course then launched into its longest stretch with holes measuring 430, 518, 428, 172, and 459 yards. Though sizable enough to grab one's attention, these holes appear to have been distinguished by little other than their brawn, a condition exacerbated by the removal of several less-than-inspiring geometric bunkers prior to or during the war years.

One particularly disappointing alteration was the aforementioned moving of the 18th green, apparently to make room for additional recreational facilities adjacent to the Jungle Club Hotel. Originally a 330-yard par-4 which twice crossed the creek, the modern version became shorter and straighter, removing nearly all interest and a great deal of challenge. Definitely not an improvement for the club's golfing guests, but a realistic concession to the distinctions between resort and country club golf.

How St. Petersburg Would Measure Up Today

As an enjoyable, historic, and very well-located resort facility. Period.

ALSO BY A.W. TILLINGHAST

Perhaps due to their inherent quality, or simply to Tillinghast's success in marketing himself into something of a brand name, this Hall-of-Fame architect's designs manage to survive in great number. Indeed, beyond those just profiled, what remains to be discussed lies as much in the area of courses planned but never built as it does with genuinely lost facilities.

Still, several that did once exist are worthy of mention, one of the earliest and most mysterious being the Atlantic Beach Country Club near Jacksonville, Florida. An amenity of the Atlantic Beach Hotel, this layout was built in 1915 (likely during the same Southern swing that produced the St. Petersburg Country Club) on land which partially overlaps today's Selva Marina Country Club. Though its par-71 layout measured only 5,936 yards, it apparently featured several fine holes, particularly the 360-yard dogleg first and the 411-yard 16th, a hole to which Tillie would later make occasional reference in his writings on architecture. Unhappily, what we don't know about this early layout vastly exceeds what we do, perhaps because by all indications it was gone—for reasons unknown—by 1920 or '21. Another oddity: the local newspaper gave great coverage to the opening of a nine-hole pitch-and-putt course (also designed by Tillinghast) but made only casual mention shortly thereafter when the full-size 18-holer debuted. Of course Tillie's well-earned reputation was not yet so imposing in 1915.

Also notable was the Country Club of Ithaca, an upstate New York facility that began with a 1920 nine-holer, then blossomed into a full 18 in 1926. Originally measuring a somewhat scrawny 5,750 yards (lengthened, by 1938, to 6,160), it was hardly Tillinghast golf on the regal scale. Yet the Ithaca course did contain many interesting and challenging holes, not the

Country Club of Ithaca layout, circa 1938. Some bunkers likely lost since the course's 1926 opening.

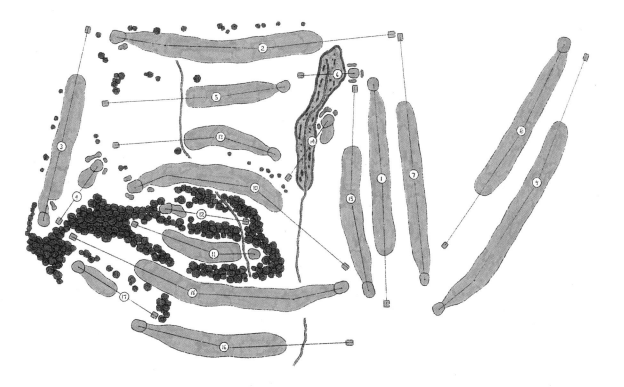

CC OF ITHACA																				
405	525	360	135	345	100	420	440	570	3300	475	270	175	320	140	380	400	190	510	2860	6160
4	5	4	3	4	3	4	4	5	36	5	4	3	4	3	4	4	3	5	35	71

least of which was the 100-yard sixth, a short pitch across a small ravine to a heavily-bunkered putting surface. Located immediately adjacent to Cornell University, this layout was affected by changes in land ownership, mandating alterations by Robert Trent Jones in 1938. Several further changes followed so that by the time the entire property was sold to the University in 1957, Tillie's early work had already become a casualty.

Though he also lost a nine-hole course in Kingsport, Tennessee, the original Mountain Ridge in New Jersey, and Cedarbrook in Philadelphia, perhaps more interesting were planned Tillinghast designs that never quite got off the drawing board.

Most notable in this regard was the Poxono Country Club, a widely-advertised project to be built adjacent to Tillie's first-ever design at Shawnee-on-Delaware, Pennsylvania. What made Poxono so fascinating were ads suggesting that the club was intended to be the architect's masterpiece, a public relations effort furthered by a November, 1926, article in *Golf Illustrated* in which he detailed several impressive-looking holes "now under construction at Poxono." Two of these, relatively short par-3s, were to be situated flush along the banks of the Delaware River with the water very much in play. What exactly sidetracked Poxono remains unknown, its dissolution coming at least a couple of years prior to the standard terminator of the period, the Depression. Extensive research has yielded no evidence of any building having actually taken place—and yet there were Tillie's words, "now under construction..."

Another unfulfilled design was the Davis Shores Country Club in St Augustine, Florida, a course intended as a centerpiece of a real estate development on Anastasia Island. That Tillie visited the area several times (including during his building of nearby Atlantic Beach) is a matter of record, as are notes on many period land plats reserving space for a golf course. Research with local planning departments and historical societies, however, confirms that the Davis Shores golf course was in fact never constructed. Like Poxono, the platting notes were dated several years ahead of the Depression (though not necessarily ahead of the Florida real estate bust) but unlike Poxono, there is little evidence to suggest any commencement of construction at that time.

As prolific a writer as Tillinghast was, there are several references throughout his work to planning courses in locales not represented among his extant facilities. Some, we can assume, never got built, while others may have enjoyed starkly abbreviated existences. But given the degree to which both he and others chronicled his finer layouts, it seems doubtful that any such facilities were on par with his best work.

The planned par-3 second at Poxono, a good one—had it ever been built.
(*Golf Illustrated*)

CAPTAIN H.C. TIPPETT

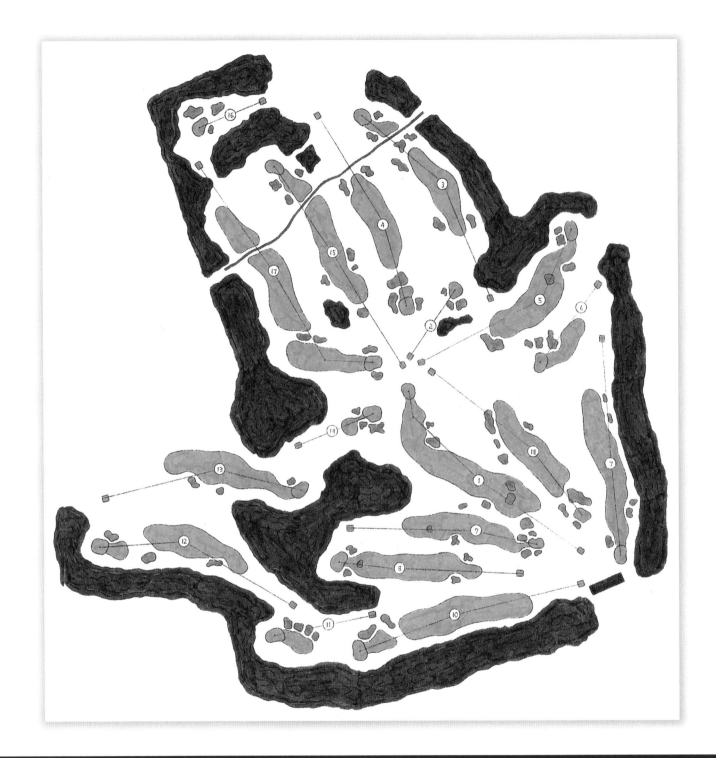

MONTAUK DOWNS																			
485	165	470	420	430	200	445	375	380	3370	465	225	430	435	165	465	130	525	430	3270	6640
5	3	5	4	4	3	4	4	4	36	5	3	4	4	3	5	3	5	4	36	72

MONTAUK DOWNS COUNTRY CLUB
MONTAUK, NY

Opened in 1927 / 6,640 yards Par-72

Numerous factors go into determining whether or not a particular area will be suitable for resort development—factors as diverse as climate, geographic proximity or isolation, amount of developable land, general marketability and many more. It is at times a complicated equation, and perhaps one capable of explaining away such adventurous-but-doomed propositions as California's Salton Sea, Virginia's Yorktown project, or North Carolina's Overhills.

Naturally, certain locations clearly seem less suited to such development, places which, like the tip of Long Island's remote Montauk Point, would otherwise appear to be on one's way to absolutely nowhere. Yet once upon a time during the Roaring Twenties, Montauk was indeed the site of one of America's grandest resort undertakings. In fact, the entire project seemed well on its way to genuine, long-term success until...

But we are getting ahead of ourselves, for the fascinating story of the Montauk Downs golf course began many years earlier in, of all places, Indianapolis. There, in the heart of the very unresort-like Rust Belt, a man by the name of Carl Fisher made a fortune in the manufacture of automobile headlights, eventually selling his company to Union Carbide and setting off after more enjoyable fields of endeavor.

Carl Fisher was a dreamer, a builder (of the Indianapolis Motor Speedway, among other things) and like most people of sound mind, a lover of the sort of warm, sunny weather not generally found in Indiana in January. Fisher thus became a regular seasonal visitor to America's first tropical winter playground, Miami, and the primary developer of its romantic and enduring offshoot, Miami Beach.

That Miami Beach was so successful seems a no-brainer, its combination of Gulfstream weather, glimmering beaches and an absolutely ideal location comprising a powerful commercial package. Though up-and-down real estate cycles and the occasional hurricane did present obstacles, Fisher forged ahead and by the mid-1920s he had created, both for himself and the South Florida region, a most famous and valuable piece of property.

Enter Montauk, New York.

The par-3 second hole, downhill and all carry. (John Keough)

The magnitude of his Miami Beach involvement having turned Fisher into a full-time Floridian, he began to view the weather question from the reverse perspective. Hot Southern summers, after all, dictated the creation of a cool-weather retreat, a new destination where his carefully managed mix of upscale hostelries, nightlife, and daytime recreational amenities would attract only the finest clientele. In short, a Miami Beach of the North.

What led Fisher to select Montauk is not entirely clear but his commitment to its full-scale development was absolute. He purchased over 9,000 acres of land for $2.5 million, then sunk another $8 million into the Montauk Manor Hotel, a yacht club, polo fields, one of the world's first indoor tennis facilities, and additional improvements.

When it came time to incorporate golf into the mix, Fisher once again called upon Captain H.C. Tippett, a transplanted Scot of little reputation but not inconsiderable design talent. A fine player himself, Tippett had long been in charge of the golfing end of Fisher's Miami Beach operation, designing such facilities as La Gorce and the long-gone Bayshore and Golf Park, the latter (located in nearby Hialeah) one of South Florida's first master-planned golf communities. As far as records tell us, Montauk Downs would be Tippett's one and only Northern design and he certainly made a fine effort of it,

The ninth green, 1931. (*Golf Illustrated*)

utilizing the rolling, links-like Long Island terrain to great advantage and, it has long been rumored, consulting with none other than Charles Blair Macdonald on its formulation.

Was Macdonald actually involved at Montauk? There exists no credible evidence either for or against, though the obvious lack of replica holes might be interpreted as suggesting not. Still, Captain Tippett's layout proved both varied and difficult, featuring large greens and a very traditional lack of trees, its flanks instead covered with sandy overgrowth and thick, jungle-like bush. Indeed, in 1928 an article appearing in *The American Golfer* called Montauk "as close an approach to the famous seaside links of the British Isles as may be had anywhwere."

The opener, a fairly simple uphill par-5, generally provided for a pleasant start, but things became immediately more engaging at the second, a pretty one-shotter of 165 yards. Played from atop an area known as "Tee Hill" (a central hilltop housing the tees of holes two, five, 15, and 18.), number two offered a panoramic view of the surrounding countryside before tumbling between grass-covered dunes to a large, particularly well-bunkered green.

Following the 470-yard par-5 third came a particularly challenging stretch featuring three especially long par-4s. The fifth, a 430-yard dogleg-left bordered by thick overgrowth, was likely the most difficult but it might have been pushed by number seven, a 445-yarder played slightly uphill with out-of-bounds guarding its entire left side.

That the seventh green returned to the clubhouse is not as odd as it may seem, for in Tippett's initial design the out-and-back eighth and ninth were actually Montauk's openers,

The short par-3 16th, with palatial Montauk Manor on the horizon. (*The American Golfer*)

resequencing the remaining outward holes so that number seven eventually closed out the nine. Given the relative tameness of these two additional par-4s, such a configuration appeared to make eminent sense and no evidence remains to suggest a reason for the change.

The back nine began with another short par-5 before launching into a second particularly difficult stretch, the backbone of which were the long par-4 12th and 13th where drives positioned on the more dangerous sides of the fairway opened up the most open angles of approach.

The 465-yard 15th was the club's fourth diminutive three-shotter—always an exciting prospect for the better player—and preceded what was surely its most photogenic hole, the 130-yard 16th. Here the player faced only a short-iron approach but one requiring precise execution, for the green was a small, elevated affair bunkered short and right and falling away elsewhere into rough and jungle. With the suitably imposing Montauk Manor Hotel perched atop a bluff on the horizon, the 16th was a frequent visitor to period magazines and brochures.

Teeing off at the 430-yard 18th, a strong finisher over Montauk's links-like terrain. (*Golf Illustrated*)

Following a long, three-shot par-5, the Montauk layout returned to the clubhouse with a final man-sized par-4, the 430-yard 18th. Playing slightly uphill, this strong finisher first required a solid tee shot over cross-bunkering, then a long-iron approach across an enormous fronting trap. Not an all-time killer, but one doesn't imagine that many matches were settled with a birdie at the last, either.

Though Carl Fisher was successful in creating a marvelously planned, amenity-filled resort community, the timing of his northern development left a great deal to be desired. Unlike Miami Beach, which was already well-established by 1929, the as-yet-inadequately-sold Montauk was ravaged by the crash of the stock market, bringing an abrupt halt to both the area's development and Carl Fisher's personal wealth.

Blessed with a temperate climate and several state and county parks, the Montauk area is considerably more successful today, but its landscape remains dotted with various leftovers of the Fisher era. Though Captain Tippett's wonderful golf course regrettably isn't one of them, golf is still played on a state-owned 1970 Robert Trent Jones layout. The new facility is quite good as modern public golf goes, but a far cry from Montauk's historic, ambiance-filled original.

How Montauk Downs Would Measure Up Today

One great thing about golf courses situated in windy locales: no matter how much technology may render an old layout obsolete, a nice, blustery afternoon can wreak havoc upon even the best player's score. In other words, even with only minimal alteration, Montauk would still retain much of its considerable challenge, requiring all manner of shots to negotiate its wildly-appealing terrain. And for the toughness-minded among us, convert two of the short par-5s into long par-4s and you'd really have something.

Not surefire Top 100 material perhaps, but Montauk Downs would absolutely have been well worth the New York city dweller's three-hour trip.

Willie Watson & Sam Whiting

OLYMPIC (Ocean)																				
455	202	338	300	138	382	465	411	528	3219	185	421	380	514	162	360	503	402	460	3387	6606
5	3	4	4	3	4	5	4	5	37	3	4	4	5	3	4	5	4	5	37	74

THE OLYMPIC CLUB
SAN FRANCISCO, CA

Ocean Course, 1924 / 6,606 yards Par-74

When pondering the great body of America's classic golf venues, one cannot help but focus upon the Eastern part of the country, for it is there that the majority of such time-proved tests reside. Of course there is very little surprising about this geographic concentration. Given the fact that what we today refer to as the Northeastern Corridor incorporated virtually all of the nation's early centers of population and wealth, it would be surprising if it had not been the breeding ground for most of golf's early North American advances.

Perhaps the one great exception to this Eastern dominance was located about as far from the great power bases of New York, Boston, Philadelphia, and the District of Columbia as one could get, some 2,500 miles west in the Bay Area of San Francisco. For here lay a sizable population and monetary center which was also blessed, perhaps since its discovery by Sir Francis Drake in 1579, with the smattering of British immigrants necessary to get the game's local popularity jump-started. The modern game of golf would not take root in America until roughly 300 years later but when it did, two of the earliest courses to be built west of the Mississippi River were located in the Bay Area: Burlingame in the San Mateo County suburb of Hillsborough (1893) and The Presidio of San Francisco (1895).

Considering this early activity, the Olympic Club was a relative latecomer to the golfing mix. Already well established as a downtown San Francisco athletic facility, the club began its post-World War I era by purchasing the 18-hole Wilfrid Reid-designed Lakeside Golf and Country Club, a 6,410-yard, par-75 course of modest repute. Not altogether satisfied with the Lakeside track, however, Olympic elected to plow the old course up and build a new 36-hole facility, the first 18 to be located primarily upon the old Lakeside site, the second straddling Skyline Boulevard and running down to the cliffs above the Pacific.

The club selected as its architect Mr. Willie Watson, late of Scotland but, by the early 1920s, firmly established as a Bay Area course designer and professional. Though Watson's architectural career was largely centered in Northern California (where the Orinda Country Club remains among his better surviving designs), records also indicate work being done in Los Angeles and throughout the Midwest, including the lost Number Two and Three courses at Olympia Fields in Chicago. Here in San Francisco, Watson enlisted Olympic's greenskeeper-to-be, Sam Whiting, as his construction supervisor, allowing for a timely building process and the opening of both courses in early 1924.

Heavily contoured ninth green—528 yards, par 5. (*Golf Architecture in America*)

Familiar to most modern-day golf fans, the Lake Course would not achieve its position of national eminence for the two decades it took for several thousand hand-planted pine, cypress, and palm trees to mature. Initially selected as the site of the 1955 U.S. Open, the Lake has since hosted Opens in 1966, 1987, and 1998, and a pair of U.S. Amateurs in 1958 and 1981. It remains ranked among America's top 20 courses in all major publications and has evolved into something of a golfer's household name.

And yet it wasn't intended as the club's marquee facility.

Strange as it may sound, it was actually the Ocean Course (also referred to as the Ocean Links) that was expected to be the club's calling card, its spectacular clifftop holes and direct exposure to the Pacific breezes making for a more exciting and traditional challenge. Tragically, due to clifftop land erosion, the Ocean's original configuration would exist for little more than a year. As a result, the finer details of its layout went almost entirely undocumented, necessitating what can only be called, over 70 years later, an educated guess as to

The 185-yard 10th, running downhill to the water's edge. (Gabriel Moulin)

some of its particulars. The routing, culled from several published sources, is relatively precise. The specific placement of hazards, however—drawn primarily from a handful of old hole photos, written descriptions, and a rudimentary preconstruction map—may contain the occasional error. But such, unfortunately, is the nature of this particular brand of archeology.

The Ocean course began on the inland side of Skyline Boulevard with its first seven holes featuring two short par-5s, a pair of sub-340-yard par-4s and a 138-yard par-3. Though each appears to have provided some particular type of challenge (the short fifth, for example, offering a small putting surface nearly surrounded by bunkers), the lone truly difficult hole amid this diminutive stretch came at the 202-yard second. Here one's approach was aimed directly into the Pacific breeze, the small, well-bunkered green likely serving as an elusive target in those days of hickory shafts and less-lively golf balls.

Now, following number seven, the golfer embarked upon a most wonderful stretch, marching first northward, then southward, through a series of six spectacular holes built upon some of golf's most wildly thrilling seaside terrain.

The 421-yard 11th, working back southward along the coastline. (*Green Book of Golf*)

The first of the bunch was the 411-yard eighth, whose native rough and stark, natural-looking design truly harkened back to the famous links of the motherland. Next came the splendid 528-yard ninth, a three-shotter requiring an accurate drive played from atop a cliff, then two more wind-resistant strokes across heavily-undulating fairway to a deep, three-tiered putting surface.

Having reached higher ground, the 185-yard 10th then plunged downward to sea level, making it one of the most beautiful par-3s ever built in America. With its green edged by two small bunkers, surrounded by native grasses and framed by both the ocean and distant Marin headlands, it genuinely looked (and played) more like some ancient Irish Coast classic than a man-made, big-city 1924 design.

The 421-yard 11th now skirted land's end, the right edge of its fairway bordered not by rough but rather by a steep hillside tumbling rather suddenly to the beach below. Any sliced tee shot was history (though in fairness, the incoming ocean breeze likely kept a good many such misses in play) and the approach was no bargain either, generally requiring a long iron carried across a rough, open patch which fronted the putting surface.

The 380-yard 12th continued in the same direction, concluding in another gorgeous green site, a small, punch-bowl-like spot pinched between the ocean and a long, steep hillside. Watson did alter the natural landscape here by adding two left-side bunkers, presumably to prevent less-bold approaches aimed safely up the hillside from bounding down onto the putting surface.

Finally, the last of the Ocean Links's great stretch came at the 514-yard 13th, a testing par-5 about which the 1924 *Green Book of Golf* stated, most succinctly, "impossible to get home in two."

The seaside green at the 12th, a 380-yard par-4 nestled snugly between the cliffs and the Pacific. (*Green Book of Golf*)

Following the short 14th, the player crossed Skyline Boulevard for the fourth and final time to face a set of finishers which, though perfectly decent, likely came as a mild let-down after so special a mid-round run. The 17th, considered little more than a drive-and-pitch at 402 yards because of the prevailing wind, may well have been the best of the bunch before the short par-5 18th offered the aggressive player the distinct opportunity to get home in two and finish in style.

The history of the Ocean Course has been a rather checkered one since those early landslides removed its best holes permanently from play. Sam Whiting performed major surgery during 1926 and '27 to reconfigure the layout away from the coastline and subsequent changes ultimately left nearly the entire track squeezed around the Lake Course on the east side of the road. In the mid-1990s new holes were rather ambitiously built upon what remains of the oceanfront land, only to be severely damaged by El Niño storms, placing the long-term usage of the property's western flank very much in question.

Regardless of future advances in course design technology, it seems impossible that the Ocean Links will ever again exist in any form closely resembling its classic original. Sad for the Olympic Club, sad for golf, and especially sad for Willie Watson, as the Ocean Links was, without question, his masterpiece.

How Olympic Would Measure Up Today

In a superficial sense this golf course could have retained virtually all of its original challenge without making a single physical change. Simply convert holes one, seven, and 18 into long par-4s and at 6,606 yards, par 71, it would be a tiger. But far more important is what the Ocean Links would represent were it still with us: a thrilling, inspiring, oceanfront design with several holes virtually indistinguishable from those of the great British links. Take a moment to formulate a list of American courses that truly fit that description.

A moment is all you'll need.

Nine Additional Lost Courses of Historic Note

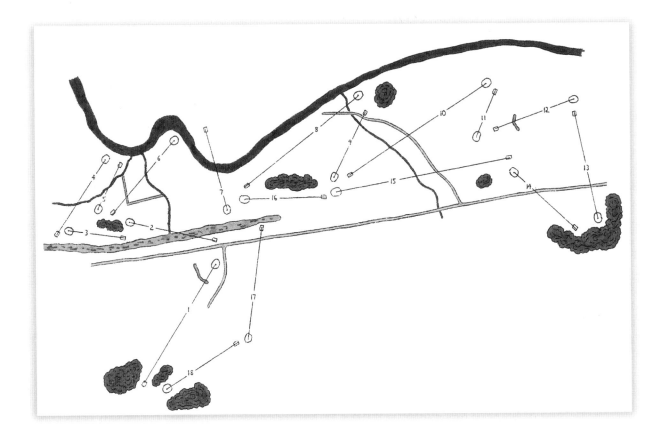

Baltimore CC's original Roland Park layout, circa 1900.

BALTIMORE																				
354	255	155	240	141	269	225	398	198	2235	468	142	257	305	227	488	220	201	235	2543	4778
4	4	3	4	3	4	4	4	3	33	5	3	4	4	4	5	4	4	4	37	70

BALTIMORE COUNTRY CLUB

Roland Park Course, Baltimore, MD

In 1898 Willie Dunn, the man who had sparked golf's Eastern growth by introducing Mssrs. Vanderbilt, Cryder, and Mead to the game in Biarritz, France, some seven years earlier, built the Roland Park Course of the Baltimore Country Club. Though a bit less spectacular than his self-proclaimed clifftop masterpiece at Ardsley, New York, the Roland Park track was certainly one of the most advanced of its day and, as site of the 1899 U.S. Open, also one of the most historic.

It was, not surprisingly, absurdly short by today's standards, its 4,778 yard, par-70 statistics not even equitable with anything resembling modern design. However, it was also a rather imaginative layout, built over tough, undulating ground and featuring several holes situated along a small river known as Jones Falls. Bunkering in the modern sense was virtually nonexistent but trees, the difficult terrain, and the then-standard assortment of ditches, stone walls, and other obstacles all conspired to create something of a thinking man's design.

Eventually lengthened to over 5,800 yards by 1912, this early classic fell victim to the expanding club's need for larger facilities, ultimately being replaced by A.W. Tillinghast's wonderful 1926 layout some eight miles away. Long but a memory, the Roland Park Course is tangibly memorialized by two of its original holes (including the scenic downhill first) which are still maintained adjacent to the original downtown clubhouse—a suitable reminder of golf's pioneer days.

Springfield, NJ

Long before modern champions did battle over its famous Lower Course (as well as before Tony Manero won the 1936 U.S. Open on the Upper), Baltusrol was constantly updating its facilities for Major Championship play. Thus were numerous permutations to their original 1895 nine-holer endured prior to settling upon an 18-hole layout which, by 1910, was widely considered among the best in the country. This 6,189-yard course occupied much of the club's familiar present-day land and hosted, among other events, the 1915 U.S. Open.

Though somewhat antiquated by today's standards, this was a well-bunkered and interesting layout featuring several notable hazards and holes. An enormous cross-bunker excavated

from the first fairway, for example, drew lots of period attention and the 520-yard par-5 16th (a hole fairly similar to the modern Lower Course 18th) was an obviously difficult test. But no hole at Baltusrol (or perhaps anywhere else) drew more attention than the 330-yard 10th, a short par-4 played downhill to one of America's earliest island greens.

By 1918 this legendary hole had been removed from play and the overall layout slightly rerouted and expanded to 6,308 yards. By 1922, when A.W. Tillinghast's classic 36-hole redesign was complete, an entirely new facility had been born.

Baltusrol's 330-yard 10th, one of golf's first island greens. (*Golf Illustrated*)

CALIFORNIA COUNTRY CLUB

Culver City, CA

In the otherwise well-recorded history of Los Angeles area golf design, the California Country Club was an oddly undocumented facility. Possibly built by Norman MacBeth (designer of nearby Wilshire Country Club) and certainly reworked by Max Behr, it was located on very hilly ground just southwest of today's Hillcrest Country Club, in the neighborhood of Cheviot Hills. Established in 1917, it was a particularly well-heeled club which catered to something of an "A-list" Hollywood clientele (a logical outgrowth of neither Los Angeles Country Club nor Bel Air accepting show business types at the time).

On paper the California layout appeared sizable at 6,538 yards, but its overall yardage was boosted considerably by a pair of especially long holes, the 560-yard ninth and 581-yard 16th. The 242-yard, par-3 seventh was equally challenging but numerous short and mid-length par-4s made California, on the whole, somewhat less demanding than many of its high-profile neighbors.

Staten Island, NY

Scottish architect Tom Bendelow, champion of the sarcastically-labeled "Eighteen Stakes on a Sunday Afternoon" school of golf design, is seldom recalled for his body of great or historic works but one exception might be Fox Hills. Constructed in the Stapleton section of New York's Staten Island in 1901, this 6,232-yard, par-73 layout was, to be sure, rather rudimentary, initially lacking any form of bunker or other man-made hazard. It did, however, feature Hell's Kitchen, a deep chasm which crossed through several back-nine holes, giving the windswept layout a good deal of challenge. Played frequently by the stars of the day, Fox Hills drew praise from the likes of Walter Travis and Harry Vardon, the latter going so far as to predict that it would someday become "the classic course in the United States."

That such was never the case may speak more to Vardon's generosity of praise than any inherent design flaws. But regardless, Fox Hills did become one of the most altered courses around, touched up by Robert White in 1924, Donald Ross in 1928, and, quite likely, several others.

Though no aerial photos are known to exist of the facility, it is interesting to note that a comparison of scorecards (upon which numerous holes retained their original names and yardages despite resequencing) strongly suggests that a good deal of Bendelow's work remained intact throughout the 1920s, likely surviving until the club's demise in the maelstrom of events surrounding World War II.

Fox Hills 18th hole, final round, 1915
Metropolitan Open. (*Golf Illustrated*)

The ninth green at Fox Hills shortly after Robert White's 1924 makeover.

The 15th at Fox Hills, also 1924.

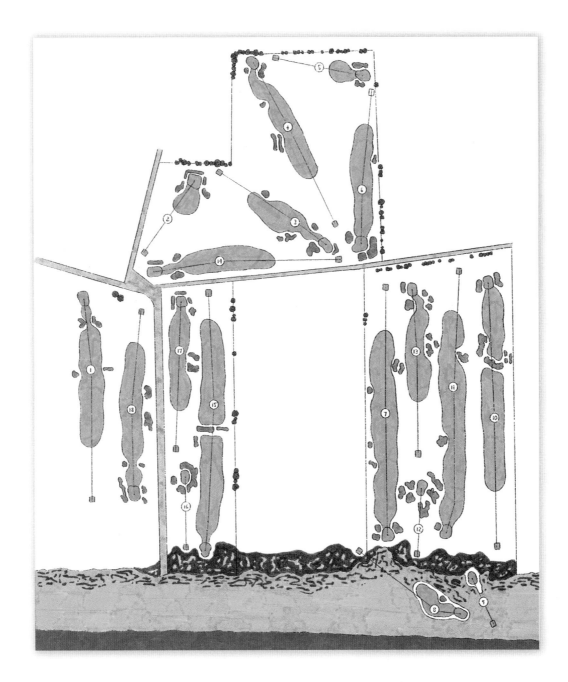

Maidstone's East Course, pre-World War II. Only nine holes remain.

MAIDSTONE																				
345	150	230	325	170	312	460	215	130	2337	470	465	135	315	325	452	135	292	350	2939	5726
4	3	4	4	3	4	5	4	3	34	5	5	3	4	4	5	3	4	4	37	71

MAIDSTONE CLUB (EAST COURSE)

East Hampton, NY

Maidstone exists today as one of America's most exclusive clubs, featuring a marvelous 18-hole course and a shorter, secondary nine which was itself an 18-holer of note prior to World War II. Laid out by Scotsman Willie Park, this second or East course at least partially utilized green sites that had originally been part of the much-altered West, but also crossed onto land leased beyond the property's eastern boundary line. Consequently, when this land was given up during the war, the club lost not a complete nine but a section of seven holes (numbers seven through 13), requiring them to combine holes two, three, and four into one to reestablish a nine-hole sequence.

Of the overall 10 holes thus lost, the best likely were a pair of particularly short ones situated among the seaside dunes, the 215-yard, two-shot eighth and the 130-yard ninth. The 135-yard 12th, played to a green engulfed by six bunkers, was also notable, as was the inland 150-yard second, an Eden-like one-shotter likely built by Seth Raynor during a brief association with the club.

Though these lost holes were hardly world-class in caliber, they were arranged in a fascinating manner and actually progressed further out into the dunes than any on the famous West layout. The area houses affluent Hamptons residences today.

Ormond Beach, FL

Located close to the hemisphere's oldest city, St. Augustine, FL, Ormond Beach was one of America's first golf resort areas, springing to life following the arrival of Henry Flagler's railroad in the mid-1890s. Though no definitive record exists as to the precise date of its construction, the golf club was designed by George Merritt and existed in association with the Hotel Ormond, long a mainstay among Flagler resort hostelries.

Laid out between the Atlantic Ocean and the Halifax River, the 5,887-yard layout was universally considered among Florida's most interesting during those early years, likely owing

to its uncommonly rolling terrain. It also included several very long holes, none more so than the 620-yard 14th, a genuine backbreaker given both the resort clientele and primitive equipment of the time.

Ormond Beach was also famous as the winter home of John D. Rockefeller, patriarch of the American family most synonymous with illustrious wealth. A thoroughly avid golfer, Rockefeller played precisely eight holes each day during Ormand's winter season, a remarkable feat for a man in his late eighties, particularly during the pre-golf cart era.

Sixth tee at Ormond Beach, one of Florida's earliest layouts and winter home of John D. Rockefeller. (*Golf Illustrated*)

PASADENA GOLF CLUB

Altadena, CA

Intended as the keystone of one of Southern California golf's more ambitious under-takings, the Pasadena Golf Club was completed in 1920 by the Chicago-based architect/professional team of George O'Neil and Jack Croke. Located slightly northeast of town in neighboring Altadena, it was planned as the first of three 18-hole facilities that would serve club members, real estate buyers, and guests of several prominent area resort hotels.

Measuring 6,291 yards while playing to a par of 70, Pasadena was both a scenically beautiful layout and a solid test, featuring several very long par-4s including the 425-yard first and 450-yard 10th. The 110-yard 14th played to a small, ravine-guarded green while the 375-yard 15th was routed along a reservoir.

Though widely profiled in the period press, the Pasadena development never approached the grandeur envisioned by its developers. Despite marvelous surroundings, warm winter weather, and a professional staff that included Leo Diegel and Eddie Loos (in addition to the designers), this original layout was eventually sold off for housing and no further golf holes were ever constructed.

1921 advertisement detailing resort golf in Pasadena. (*Golf Illustrated*)

Tuxedo Park, NY

Located some 20 miles northwest of New York City, the Tuxedo development was organized in 1885 as a sporting retreat for some of New York society's finest. Originally intended as a hotbed of hunting and fishing, the community saw the debut of golf with a thoroughly rudimentary six-hole layout in 1889, then moved more formally into the game with subsequent nine-hole layouts in 1892 and 1894. Though exact date and architect are unknown, this latest nine was expanded to 18 at some point prior to 1900 and prospered, with only modest alteration, thereafter.

Noted for its great difficulty, the course crossed Tuxedo Brook several times and, according to an 1895 issue of *Scribner's*, offered "great variety in its hazards of hills, stone walls, railroad embankments lined with blast furnace slag, apple trees…" and so on. Though not terribly long, it did include the 425-yard par-4 14th, known as "Rifle Gallery" for the tremendous length and accuracy required of its tee shot.

Never selected for national tournament play, Tuxedo did host the 1902 Metropolitan Amateur (won by the great Walter Travis) along with several other regional events. This dangerous old relic met its end in 1953 when New York State elected to route its new Thruway through the area, prompting the club to hire Robert Trent Jones to build a distinctly more modern layout on land nearby.

APPENDIXES

APPENDIXES

I. The Author's Choice

America's 18 Greatest Lost Holes

#9 Boca Raton Resort & Club (South) 555 yds, Par-5
A long three-shotter every bit as treacherous as its more celebrated sister 17th. Countless angles for drives and seconds, particularly if one wished to approach from the optimum right side of the fairway.

#17 Boca Raton Resort & Club (South) 570 yds, Par-5
A replica of Pine Valley's Hell's Half Acre seventh and not much easier. Almost surely a three-shot "untouchable" during its too-brief existence.

#4 The Lido GC 466 yds, Par-5
In 1915 C.B Macdonald called it the finest of its type in the world—and who would argue? Likely one of golf's 18 best-ever holes, alive or dead.

#9 The Olympic Club (Ocean) 528 yds, Par-5
A long and spectacular clifftop hole played to a deep, three-tiered green. Some days reachable in two, other days untouchable, all depending upon that ever-present wind.

#9 Gibson Island GC 330 yds, Par-4
One of golf's least-known great holes despite its sensational waterfront location. A strategic gem and proof once again of the short par-4's unique value.

#10 Key West GC 340 yds, Par-4
Even more spectacular than Gibson Island, its island green making a tantalizing target only 235 yards away via the direct route, or with a more conventional drive-and-pitch approach.

#16 La Cumbre CC 416 yds, Par-4
Another breathtaking green site, the putting surface wedged between wild hillside and deep, rock-strewn canyon. With layup area provided short-left, truly one of America's greatest-ever strategic holes.

#12 The Lido GC 433 yds, Par-4
As difficult a driving hole as has ever been built, doglegging right around the lagoon, the prevailing left-to-right wind blowing one's ball toward disaster.

#15 The Lido GC 404 yds, Par-4
Less famous than the nearby 18th but almost as strategic. Enormous fairway offered distinctly different lines of second-shot attack depending upon the gutsiness of one's tee shot.

#18 The Lido GC 424 yds, Par-4
Dr. MacKenzie's prize-winner and, in its time, the world's most famous alternate-fairway hole. Widely thought of as The Lido's best.

#7 Oakland GC 385 yds, Par-4
An early version of target golf with both drive and approach crossing a deep ravine in order to reach their targets.

#10 Sharp Park 392 yds, Par-4
MacKenzie finally builds his own double-fairway hole and it becomes a genuine (though short-lived) classic.

#11 Timber Point GC 460 yds, Par-4
Charles Alison's tribute to MacKenzie's split-fairway innovation. Surely the toughest of the alternate-fairway bunch.

#18 Westhampton CC (Oneck) 430 yds, Par-4
Likely the best and most demanding two-shot Road Hole ever built in America—and what a seaside location!

#5 El Caballero CC 144 yds, Par-3
A starkly beautiful canyon-top hole played to a uniquely angled putting surface. Has a green this size ever looked so small?

#8 The Lido GC 234 yds, Par-3
Against tough competition, likely the finest Biarritz replica done in America. Waste and beach bunkering (not the usual geometric hazards) gave an aesthetic edge.

#3 Gibson Island GC 181 yds, Par-3
Possibly not the finest (reverse) Redan ever built but almost certainly the most spectacular and intimidating.

George Thomas's third at Ojai, its green surrounded by trouble. (Chisolm)

#3 Ojai Valley Inn & Club 190 yds, Par-3
A lost classic from this still-extant George Thomas design, this California one-shotter featured bunkers short, a ravine left, O.B. right, and great scenery to boot. Might leave the ranks of the lost when long-rumored restoration takes place.

And in the Afternoon (A Second 18)...
#5 Fresh Meadow CC 578 yds, Par-5
#6 The Lido GC 493 yds, Par-5
#4 Meadowbrook Hunt Club 470 yds, Par-5
#6 Oakland GC 445 yds, Par-5
#3 Beaver Tail GC 366 yds, Par-4

#6 Boca Raton Resort & Club (South) 330 yds, Par-4
#6 Fresh Meadow CC 428 yds, Par-4
#18 Deepdale GC 420 yds, Par-4
#18 Mill Road Farm GC 465 yds, Par-4
#18 Montauk Downs GC 430 yds, Par-4
#3 Oakland GC 435 yds, Par-4
#15 Shinnecock Hills GC 335 yds, Par-4
#16 Yorktown GC 316 yds, Par-4
#5 Sharp Park GC 338 yds, Par-4
#10 Gibson Island GC 220 yds, Par-3
#12 Grassy Sprain GC 245 yds, Par-3
#3 The Lido GC 175 yds, Par-3
#13 The Links Club 221 yds, Par-3

Nine Lost Classics Not Otherwise Mentioned

#13 Old CC - Flushing, NY, 310 yds, Par-4 (Emmet) - A short but spectacular hole culled from yet another of Queens' lost prewar courses. Little room for wayward iron play here as the small, elevated green was completely surrounded by 15-foot-deep bunkers.

#18 Lake Merced G&CC - Daly City, CA, 425 yds, Par-4 (MacKenzie) - A slight dogleg left played to a green perched above a small ravine, with two bunkers guarding the favored right side of the fairway. Replaced when construction of the 280 Freeway mandated a major redesign in 1960.

#7 Broadmoor CC - Colorado Springs, CO, 240 yds, Par-3 (Ross) - A man-sized one-shotter (even allowing for thinner air) following a favored Ross pattern, the green placed beyond a line of bunkers angled left-to-right. Lost when Trent Jones expanded the original layout to 36.

#6 Mid-Pacific CC - Kailua, HI, 130 yds, Par-3 (Raynor) - A then-avant garde version of the Short hole, played to an island green in the middle of Kaelepulu Stream. Green site still utilized by a thoroughly redesigned par-5 fifth.

#17 Los Angeles CC - Los Angeles, CA, 128 yds, Par-3 (Thomas) A short-lived hole of immense difficulty played across a barranca to a tiny, steeply contoured green. Removed after the 1926 Los Angeles Open when four-putts and eights were recorded.

Old 17th hole, North Course,
Los Angeles Country Club. Reaching the
putting surface hardly ended the challenge.
(*Golf Illustrated*)

#13 San Francisco GC - San Francisco, CA, 118 yds, Par-3 (Tillinghast) - "Little Tilly" was a heavily bunkered hole and the perfect complement lengthwise to San Francisco's varied other par-3s. Lost to freeway construction (see #18, Lake Merced).

#14 Engineers CC - Roslyn, NY, 105 yds, Par-3 (Herbert Strong) - Known as the "Two or 20" hole, this monster featured a tiny green flanked by sand and a steep fallaway, causing both Jones and Sarazen to record double-figure numbers here once-upon-a-time. Recently restored but not played on a regular basis.

#2 Pelham CC - Pelham, NY, 310 yds, Par-4 (Emmet) - A 90-degree dogleg left that could be driven, provided one carried a portion of the residential neighborhood that occupied the corner. Gene Sarazen closed out Walter Hagen in the finals of the 1923 PGA here by pitching his second stiff on the match's 38th hole.

#12 Bel-Air CC - Los Angeles, CA, 379 yds, Par-4 (Thomas) - The "Mae West" hole featured two very large mounds at the front corners of the green, suggesting a drive faded dangerously along a canyon wall if an unobscured second was to be had. The hole still exists, but is pointless without its long-removed natural assets.

Nine Classics Killed for Major Tournament Play

#5 Oak Hill CC (East) - Rochester, NY, 440 yds, Par-4 - Surely one of Donald Ross's best-ever par-4s, this creek-menaced hole was converted into two shorter ones in preparation for the 1980 PGA.

#10 Pebble Beach GL - Pebble Beach, CA, 436 yds, Par-5 - This spectacular hole, played to the present 10th green from a tee sited on the ocean side of the original 9th green, was rerouted during H. Chandler Egan's redesign prior to the 1929 U.S. Amateur.

#16 Augusta National GC - Augusta, GA, 145 yds, Par-3 - A tricky pitch played from alternate tees to a small, creek-guarded green. Replaced entirely in 1947 with today's more television-friendly version.

#10 Baltusrol GC - Springfield, NJ, 330 yds, Par-4 - This controversial downhiller, played to one of golf's earliest island greens, was buried during a 1916 reconfiguration.

#8 Inverness Club - Toledo, OH, 212 yds, Par-3 - An excellent Donald Ross one-shotter that was replaced prior to the 1979 U.S. Open with a par-5 known far more for Lon Hinkle's famous shortcut (and the USGA-added tree which closed it) than anything in the hole's design.

#15 Medinah CC - Medinah, IL, 315 yds, Par-4 - This wooded drive-and-pitch was the closest thing to subtle on an otherwise brutish Medinah track. Swallowed up by the present-day 14th in a 1986 U.S. Open-oriented redesign.

#4 Colonial CC - Ft. Worth, TX, 148 yds, Par-3 - An attractive, pond-fronted one-shotter that was replaced by the dull-but-difficult modern fourth in preparation for the 1941 U.S. Open.

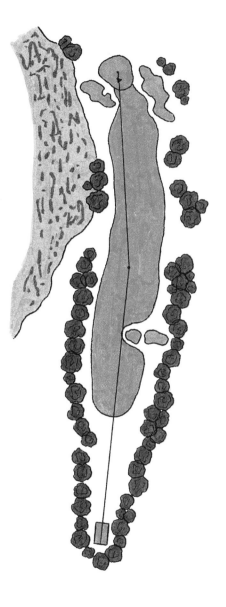

The eighteenth at Lake Merced: another beauty lost to postwar freeway expansion.

#7 Inverness Club - Toledo, OH 316 yds, Par-4 - A strategic dogleg left inviting one to go directly for the green, as eventual champion Ted Ray did four times during the 1920 U.S. Open. Also devoured by the infamous "Hinkle Tree" par-5.

#18 Congressional CC - Bethesda, MD 190 yds, Par-3 - A member of a special category—"Holes Skipped Entirely for Major Tournament Play"—until the USGA "rediscovered" it for the 1997 U.S. Open. Still very much alive—most of the time.

Nine Most Historic Lost-Course Moments

Fresh Meadow CC - Gene Sarazen's shoots a record final-round 66 to capture the 1932 U.S. Open, his fourth Major Championship.

Chicago GC - The great Harry Vardon wins his only U.S. Open title in 1900.

Oakland GC - America's first great player, Walter Travis, plays his first round of golf (at age thirty-five) in 1896.

Chicago GC - H.J. Whigham becomes the first two-time U.S. Amateur champion, successfully defending his 1896 title (won at Shinnecock Hills) here in 1897.

Atlantic City CC - Walter Travis wins his second of three U.S. Amateurs in 1901, defending the crown he'd won at Garden City a year earlier.

Pomonok CC - Henry Picard stymies Byron Nelson at the 36th hole, then utilizes a controversial free lift to win the 1939 PGA in a play-off.

Fresh Meadow - Tommy Armour wins his only PGA Championship in 1930.

Chicago GC - H. Chandler Egan becomes the U.S. Amateur's third two-time winner in 1905, successfully defending his 1904 crown won at Baltusrol.

Yorktown CC - America wins the Revolutionary War.

Nine Classics That Never Were
(Great Layouts Planned—But Never Constructed—by Master Designers)

Baltimore CC - Timonium, MD - Along with his wonderfully-unaltered East Course (built in 1926), A.W. Tillinghast gave Baltimore plans for an additional or "West" 18. Perhaps for economic reasons these plans went unused at the time—and again when the club built a distinctly modern layout on the site in 1962.

Cypress Point Club - Pebble Beach, CA - Often forgotten in the Cypress Point story is the plan that Seth Raynor produced for the club prior to his death in 1926. It was never utilized of course, but the thought of an Alps, Redan, or Biarritz routed among the dunes remains forever tantalizing.

Fairyland CC - Lookout Mountain, GA - Though very much still in business, this spectacular mountaintop Seth Raynor design had much of its planned grandeur washed away during construction. The layout which resulted (today's Lookout Mountain GC) is but a shadow of Raynor's wild original plan—though some restoration work has been undertaken.

Fishers Island GC - Fishers Island, NY - In addition to building its enduring seaside classic, Seth Raynor also provided the Fishers Island club with a routing for a second, even more spectacular layout. Utilizing land to the west of the present-day clubhouse, this track would have measured roughly 6,600 yards and featured a run of seven consecutive back-nine holes built along the shoreline of Block Island Sound. The land was instead subdivided for homesites.

Gibson Island GC - Gibson Island, MD - A similar scenario to Fishers Island, only C.B. Macdonald may have determined a routing here prior to Raynor's filling in the details. Unbuilt for Depression-era economic reasons (see page 85).

Poxono CC - Shawnee-On-Delaware, PA - The riverfront site, bold advertisements and prominent articles all suggested that this really might have been A.W. Tillinghast's masterpiece—had it ever been built (see page 176).

Riviera CC - Pacific Palisades, CA - Though it remained long-forgotten until recent years, George Thomas did in fact draw plans for a second 18 at Riviera back in the mid-1920s. This "North Course" was to be routed northeast of the present layout and was likely intended as a gentler, member-oriented facility. The land instead became the Riviera Polo Club, then later a school and residential neighborhood.

Rockwook Hall CC - Tarrytown, NY - When Devereux Emmet was engaged to build a private club on the wonderfully-beautiful William Rockefeller estate, he presented plans for 36 holes. When the club had early financial difficulties, however, the second 18 never came to fruition.

Yorktown CC - Yorktown, VA - Planned for the less-historic but more heavily wooded western side of the Yorktown property, William Flynn's 6,177-yard Lake View design never became a reality. Sad, as it likely would have been the better of a fine resort pair (see page 65).

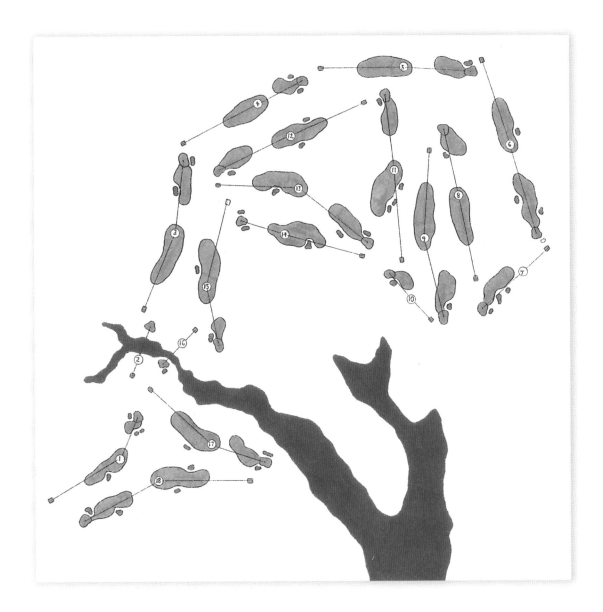

Author's rendition of William Flynn's unbuilt Lake View layout of the Yorktown
Country Club, a fine resort track routed over heavily wooded terrain.

YORKTOWN																				
327	131	415	327	392	456	225	400	438	3111	170	404	402	453	320	365	123	387	442	3066	6177
4	3	4	4	4	5	3	4	4	35	3	4	4	5	4	4	3	4	4	35	70

Nine Courses Meriting Consideration for This Book Despite Still Very Much Existing

Ardsley CC - Ardsley, NY - Traded in Willie Dunn and Dr. MacKenzie for Trent Jones.

Augusta National GC - Augusta, GA - At least the routing's still (mostly) the same.

Bel Air CC - Los Angeles, CA - Have reworked only their best holes.

Congressional CC - Bethesda, MD - Emmet would not recognize the place.

Engineers CC - Roslyn, NY - One of America's best before alterations.

La Cumbre CC - Santa Barbara, CA - For the 16th hole alone...

Lake Merced G&CC - Daly City, CA - Freeway construction.

Medinah CC (No. 3) - Medinah, IL - The 2003 U.S. Open went to Olympia Fields anyway.

Pelham CC - Pelham, NY - Decimated by Interstate 95.

Some Individual Awards

Best Lost Clubhouse - Lake Norconian Club, Norco, CA.

Shortest-Lived Course - Ocean Links (The Olympic Club).
    Special Mention - Sharp Park (precise date of obliteration unknown).
        - Key West CC (partially gone after two years).

Toughest Start - Mill Road Farm CC.

Toughest Finish - Mill Road Farm CC.

Toughest Stretch - Timber Point holes 10 through 15.

Best Par-3s - The Lido.

Best Par-4s - The Lido.

Best Par-5s - Boca Raton (South).

Best Redan - #3 Gibson Island (reverse Redan).

Best Biarritz - #8 The Lido.

The opulent clubhouse of the Lake Norconian Club, Norco, California.
(Golf Illustrated)

Best Eden - #3 The Lido.

Best Short - #8 Gibson Island.

Best Alps - #10 The Lido.

Longest Legitimate Hole - #14 Ormond Beach (620 yds).

Shortest Legitimate Hole - #6 CC of Ithaca (100 yds).

Most Destructive Single Force (Tie) - The Meadowbrook Parkway (killed the Meadowbrook Hunt Club and Old Westbury) and the Long Island Expressway (killed Deepdale, and hastened Oakland's demise).

Best Blown Chance at History - The Meadowbrook Hunt Club. Had the membership taken an interest in Horace Hutchinson's 1887 golf exhibition, they (and not St. Andrew's) could have been America's oldest enduring club.

Most Famous Ex-Clubhouse Resident - Edgar Rice Burroughs (El Caballero).

Worst Straying from Original Plans - Gibson Island.

Most Mysterious - The Royal Palms (only known documentation: the *Golf Architecture In America* photo—which didn't even know the course's name).

II. New York, Chicago & Los Angeles Maps

As accurately as possible, these maps provide the former locations of prominent lost courses within and around America's three largest cities. Because these areas frequently were dotted with short-lived, highly rudimentary facilities around the turn of the century, these maps by no means feature every known course but only those deemed to be of regulation size and/or some historical significance.

Queens/Brooklyn

1. **Old CC (Queens) - 5,904 yds Par-71**
   Located north of Northern Boulevard, on or near the site of today's Flushing Airport. Expanded from nine to 18 by Devereux Emmet in 1923.

2. **Malba Field Club (Queens) - 2,500 yds Par-32**
   A pretty nine-holer located just south of the Whitestone Bridge.

3. **Bayside Golf Links, Bayside (Page 106)**

4. **Belleclaire G&CC (Queens) - 6,218 yds Par-71**

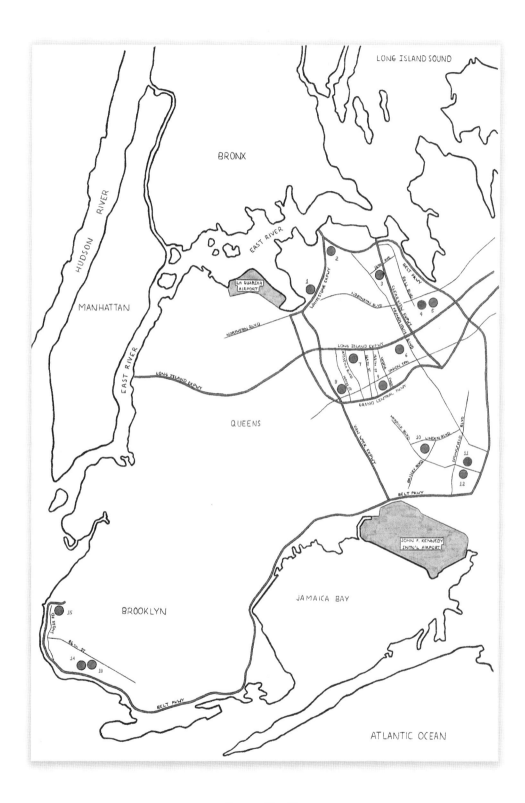

Queens/Brooklyn

Located just west of the Oakland GC, this 1919 Tom Wells design was the forerunner of today's nearby Douglaston GC and Long Island's North Hills CC.

5. **Oakland GC, Bayside (Page 118)**

6. **Fresh Meadow CC, Flushing (Page 154)**

7. **Pomonok CC, Flushing (Page 40)**

8. **Queens Valley CC, Kew Gardens (Page 47)**

9. **Hillcrest GC (Queens) - 6,210 yds Par-72**
A 1923 Devereux Emmet layout located south of Union Turnpike, on land now occupied by St. Johns University.

10. **St Albans CC, St Albans (Page 164)**

11 & 12. **Laurelton GC (Queens) - North Course: 6,277 yds Par 72**
South Course: 6,178 yds Par-73
Emmet layouts opened in 1924 and '25 on land straddling Merrick Boulevard.

13. **Marine & Field GC (Brooklyn) - Early 9 holes**
An early nine-holer which eventually combined with Dyker Meadow. Located in the northeastern section of today's Dyker Beach Park.

14. **Dyker Meadow GC (Brooklyn) - Early 9 holes 3,003 yds**
A nineteenth century Bendelow nine located on the western side of Dyker Beach Park, running to the shoreline of Gravesend Bay.

15. **Crescent AC (Brooklyn)**
One of New York's earliest clubs, Crescent occupied extraordinarily valuable land near Owl's Head Park in Bay Ridge. Built up to 18 holes by the turn of the century, the club eventually moved onto a Huntington, Long Island site.

Long Island

1. **Sound View CC, Great Neck - 6,050 yds Par-76**
An historic early club located on the southwest edge of Great Neck Peninsula, in the present-day Great Neck Estates.

2. **Deepdale GC, Great Neck (Page 76)**

3. **Glen Oaks G&CC, Great Neck - 6,212 yds Par-72**
Located just southwest of Deepdale on part of the Vanderbilt estate, this underrated

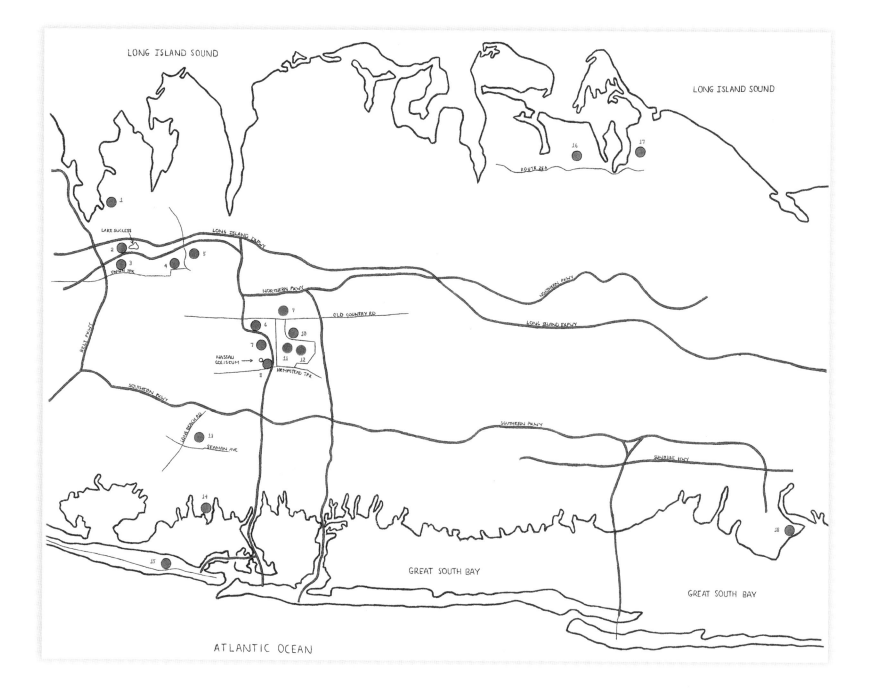

Long Island

1925 Pipe Follett design was sold for development in the 1960s.

4. **The Links GC, Roslyn (Page 94)**

5. **Shelter Rock CC, Searingtown - 6,111 yds Par-72**
    Another low-key facility positioned east of Shelter Rock Road, near the Links Club.

6. **Old Westbury GC, Garden City (Page 46)**

7. **Meadowbrook Hunt Club, Westbury (Page 36)**

8. **Coldstream CC, Hempstead - 6,490 yds Par-72**
    A 1925 Devereux Emmet design located west of today's Meadowbrook Parkway, near Nassau Coliseum, just south of the old Meadowbrook Hunt Club.

9-12. **Salisbury CC, East Meadow (Page 46)**

13. **Milburn CC, Baldwin - 6,200 yds Par-72**
    A little-known club located north of Seaman Avenue and east of Long Beach Road.

14. **Oceanside G&CC, Oceanside - 6,145 yds Par-71**
    Located on the site of today's Middle Bay CC, this host of the 1938 Metropolitan PGA disappeared after being condemned for public land usage in 1951.

15. **The Lido GC, Lido Beach (Page 88)**

16. **Huntington Crescent Club (West), Huntington (Page 45)**

17. **Northport CC, Northport - 6,321 yds Par-73**
    A 1921 Devereux Emmet design located farther out on Long Island than most.

18. **Timber Point GC, Great River (Page 28)**

Westchester

1) **Rockwood Hall GC, Tarrytown (Page 45)**

2) **Fairview CC, Elmsford - 6,018 yds Par-71**
    Original course of a club now operating in Connecticut. A 1912 Donald Ross layout located south of Grasslands Road, west of Saw Mill River Road (near the New York City water aqueduct).

3) **Old Oaks CC (West), Purchase - 3,005 yds Par-35**
    The lost third nine of this still-prominent club was sacrificed to the construction of

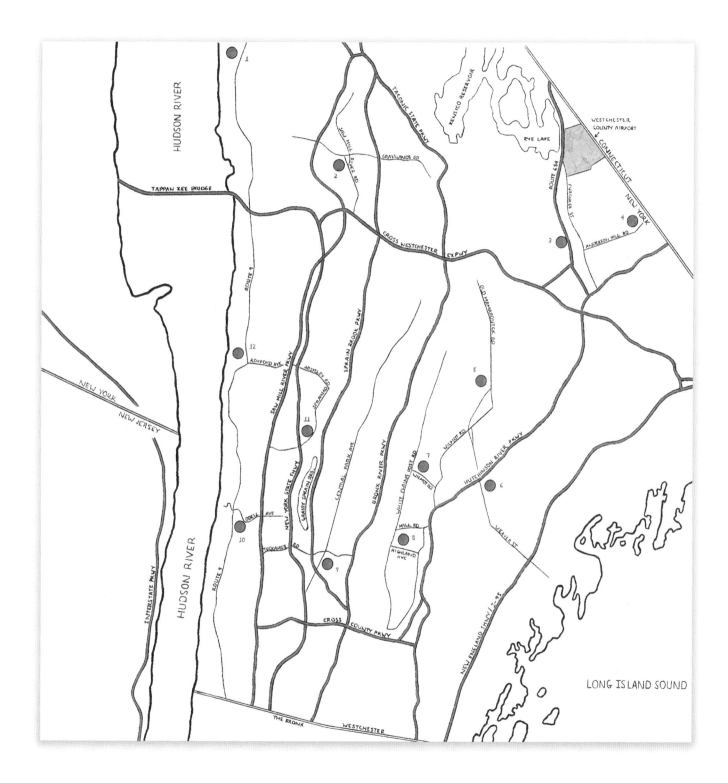

Westchester

Route 684. Tillinghast's design, C.H. Alison's construction.

4. **Purchase CC, Purchase - 6,010 yards Par-70**
Originally known as Kings Ridge, this hilly but basic layout has since been replaced by today's Doral Greens Golf Club.

5. **Fenimore GC, Scarsdale - 6,300 yds Par-73**
Forerunner of the present-day Fenway GC, on the same site. Built by Devereux Emmet in 1922.

6. **Broadmoor CC, New Rochelle - 6,271 yds Par-71**
Yet another extinct Emmet creation located just east of Weaver Street and south of the Hutchinson River Parkway, nearly adjacent to Quaker Ridge CC.

7. **Mount Vernon CC, Tuckahoe - 6,219 yds Par-71**
This layout, the successor to an early nine-holer used by both the Siwanoy and Sunningdale clubs during their formative years, was located just north of today's Lake Isle Park course, east of White Plains Road.

8. **Oak Ridge CC, Tuckahoe - 6,350 yds Par-70**
A rare lost Walter Travis design located east of White Plains Post Road and south of Mill Road.

9. **Grassy Sprain CC, Bronxville (Page 46)**

10. **Hudson River CC, Yonkers (Page 137)**

11. **St. Andrew's GC, Hastings-on-Hudson (Page 198)**

12. **Ardsley CC, Ardsley-on-Hudson - 6,338 yds Par-72**
Still-extant club's original layout, overlooking the Hudson River west of present-day course. Willie Dunn's self-proclaimed masterpiece, later reworked by Dr. MacKenzie.

Los Angeles

1. **El Caballero CC, Tarzana (Page 20)**

2. **Hollywood CC, Studio City - 6,300 yds Par-70**
Located along Ventura Boulevard, east of Coldwater Canyon Road, in the foothills of the Santa Monica Mountains.

3. **Westwood Public GC, Beverly Hills - 6,120 yds Par-71**
A frequently-praised layout located southwest of the intersection of Santa Monica and Wilshire Boulevards, near Beverly Hills High School.

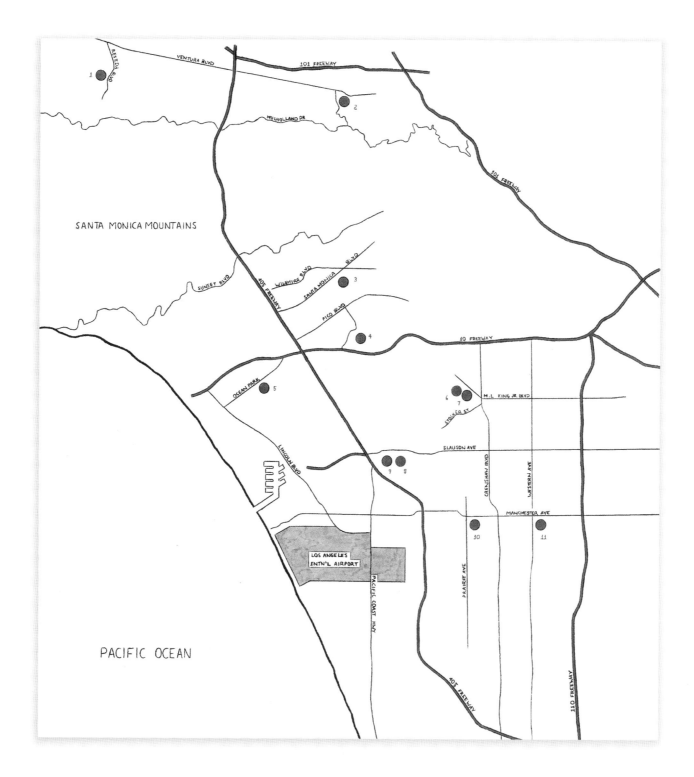

Los Angeles

4. **California CC, Culver City (Page 191)**

5. **Santa Monica Municipal, Santa Monica - 6,325 yds Par-71**
   The successor to three very rudimentary nine-holers in Santa Monica. Sat on the north side of the present Santa Monica Airport.

6 & 7. **Sunset Fields CC, Los Angeles (Page 25)**

8 & 9. **Fox Hills CC, Culver City (Page 142)**

10. **Inglewood CC, Inglewood - 6,328 yds Par-71**
   A tightly-routed track located on land that today includes the Los Angeles Forum. Hosted the 1955 Los Angeles Open.

11. **Portrero CC, Inglewood - 6,438 yds Par-72**
   A 1909 Robert Johnstone design located at 1640 East Manchester Avenue, east of Western Avenue.

12. **Redondo Beach CC, Redondo Beach - 3,055 yds Par-36**
   Likely built by Tom Bendelow, this short-lived 1911 nine-holer enjoyed a strong reputation due to its oceanfront location along today's Redondo State Beach.

Chicago

1. **Mill Road Farm GC, Lake Forest (Page 56)**

2. **Deerfield CC, Deerfield**
   Located east of Waukegan Road, north of Deerfield Road.

3. **Michigan Shores GC, Wilmette**
   A 1940s-era addition located on lakefront land presently housing Gillson Park.

4. **Dempster GC, Evanston**
   An early Tom Bendelow nine-holer located south of Dempster Street and east of Prairie Road.

5. **Bunker Hill GC, Niles - 6,387 yds Par-71**
   Located south of Dempster Street and east of Caldwell Avenue, this land was ultimately incorporated into the Clayton Smith Forest Preserve.

6. **Edgewater GC, Chicago - 6,600 yds Par-73**
   Located near the intersection of Pratt Avenue and Ridge Boulevard, Edgewater was the spawning ground for U.S. Open and two-time U.S. Amateur champ Chick Evans.

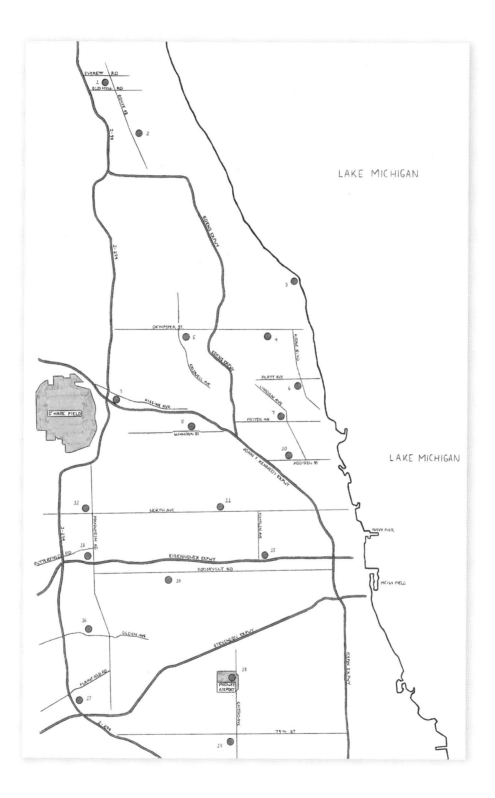

Chicago

7. **Budlong Woods GC, Chicago - 6,485 yds Par-73**
Located at the intersection of Lincoln and Balmoral Avenues, slightly northwest of Lincoln Park

8. **Big Oaks GC, Norwood Park - 6,470 yds Par-72**
An Edward Dearie-designed track located north of Gunnison Street, slightly north of Ridgemoor Country Club.

9. **Greenview GC, Chicago - 6,344 yds Par-74**
This former Chicago municipal facility was located south of Higgins Avenue, just east of O'Hare Field.

10. **Mid-City GC, Chicago - 6,040 yds Par-71**
The original configuration of this 1924 William Langford layout was short-lived, the construction of Lane Technical HS causing Langford to turn it into a pseudo-executive course in 1931.

11. **Galewood GC, Oak Park**
Located north of North Avenue, west of Central Avenue.

12. **Westward Ho GC, Melrose Park - 6,547 yds Par-71**
Located just west of Mannheim Road, this 1923 layout hosted the 1947 Chicago Victory Tournament, won by Ben Hogan.

13. **Maywood GC, Hillside - 6,406 yds Par-72**
Located on the west side of Mannheim Road, this 1923 Tom Bendelow design was distinctly modern, featuring a rare island green and heavy bunkering.

14. **Harlem GC, Forest Park - 5,949 yds Par-70**
Located west of Harlem Avenue and south of Roosevelt Road, this 1910 Tom Bendelow layout was Chicago's first privately owned public-access facility.

15. **Garfield Park GC, Chicago**
A 1908 Tom Bendelow nine-holer located north of the Eisenhower Expressway, where Jackson Avenue cuts across Garfield Park.

16. **Edgewood Valley GC, La Grange - 6,350 yds Par-70**
This 1926 William Diddel design (located just north of Ogden Avenue) was one of this established architect's earliest.

17. **Acacia CC, La Grange - 6,500 yds Par-72**
This William Langford design was located northeast of I-294 to the west of Wolf Road.

18. Laramie GC, Chicago - 6,493 yds Par-72
This private-then-public Harry Collis-designed facility was consumed by the expansion of today's Midway Aiport.

19. Golfmoor GC, Chicago - 6,400 yds Par-72
This South Side facility (located at 5000 West 79th St.) was known area-wide for its tough "horseshoe" 16th hole.

ACKNOWLEDGMENTS

No book of this sort could ever be completed without the help of far too many sources to list completely, however...

I must first thank several who were truly indispensable, including Saundra Sheffer and Marge Dewey at the R. W. Miller Golf Library, my regular Tuesday game, and whose contributions to both this volume and the world of golf research are far too numerous to count; Debbie Lelansky at the National Archives and Records Administration, who always located the golf courses even when my maps didn't; Geoff Shackelford, who, among his many contributions, got me back to writing about golf in the first place; Patty Moran and Nancy Stulack at the USGA, whose long-distance help has been constant and unfailing; and especially to my father, who took on an enormous amount of East Coast research and refused to compromise, even when I was ready to.

Also, in alphabetical order...George Bahto (the Macdonald/Raynor expert), Sandra Barghini, H.P. Boyle, Jr., Joyce Connelly and Catherine Lipper (Frederick L. Olmsted National Historic Site), David Goddard, Jeff Gottlieb, Gil Hanse, John Hyslop, Khris Januzik (Given Memorial Library), John Keough, Gerd Koenig, The Lake Forest Historical Society, Michael LaRosa, Midge Laughlin (St. Petersburg Museum of History), Carl Lind and Vinnie Leogrande (Suffolk County Planning Department), Sue Maden, Peggy McCall (Boca Raton Historical Society), Ronald A Michne Jr. (Westhampton Beach Historian), Mike Miller, Bob Mosteller (Lake County, Illinois Planning Department), Gib Papazian, The Pinehurst Resort & Country Club, Peter J. Pino, Dr. William Quirin, Kent Schwab, Jane M. Sundberg (Cultural Specialist, National Parks Service, Yorktown, Virginia), Larry Youngs and, closer to home, Kurt Wohlgemuth, Meredith Dodd, and all who have been so supportive at The Riviera Country Club (you know who you are).

Also, thanks to Lynne Johnson, Sally Casper and Danny Freels at Sleeping Bear Press, and especially to Midnight — a better friend no man has ever had.

Finally, I offer my deepest gratitude to my parents, Hannan and Roberta, whose 110% support of this book truly represents only the tip of the iceberg.

— DW